SCOTNOTE
Number 16

Liz Lochhead's

Mary Queen of Scots Got Her Head Chopped Off

Margery Palmer McCulloch

Association for Scottish Literary Studies 2000

Published by
Association for Scottish Literary Studies
c/o Department of Scottish History
9 University Gardens
University of Glasgow
Glasgow G12 8QH

www.asls.org.uk

First published 2000
Reprinted 2003, 2004 (twice), 2007

A CIP catalogue for this title is available from the British Library

ISBN 978 0 948877 39 1

The Association for Scottish Literary Studies
is in receipt of subsidy from the Scottish Arts Council

Typeset by Roger Booth Associates, Hassocks, West Sussex
Printed by Ritchie (UK) Ltd, Kilmarnock

EDITORS' FOREWORD

The *Scotnotes* booklets are a series of study guides to major Scottish writers and literary texts that are likely to be elements within literature courses. They are aimed at senior pupils in secondary schools and students in further education colleges of education. Each booklet in the series is written by a person who is not only an authority on the particular writer or text but also experienced in teaching at the relevant levels in schools or colleges. Furthermore, the editorial board, composed of members of the Schools and Further Education Committee of the Association for Scottish Literary Studies, considers the suitability of each booklet for the students in question.

For many years there has been a shortage of readily accessible critical notes for the general student of Scottish literature. *Scotnotes* has grown as a series to meet this need, and provides students with valuable aids to the understanding and appreciation of the key writers and major texts within the Scottish literary tradition.

Lorna Borrowman Smith
Ronald Renton

SCOTNOTES

Study guides to major Scottish writers and literary texts

Produced by the Schools and Further Education Committee
of the Association for Scottish Literary Studies

Original cover design by Linda Cochrane

CONTENTS

ABBREVIATIONS

BT   *Brecht on Theatre*
GGB   *The Gude and Godlie Ballatis*
JTB   *Jock Tamson's Bairns*
LLV   *Liz Lochhead's Voices*
M   *Meantime: Looking Forward to the Millennium*
PPP   *Poem, Purpose and Place*
TV   *Talking Verse*

MARY QUEEN OF SCOTS GOT HER HEAD CHOPPED OFF

INTRODUCTION

1 The Author

Liz Lochhead was born in Motherwell in 1947 and brought up from the age of four in the neighbouring mining village of Newarthill. In 'A Protestant Girlhood', her contribution to the anthology *Jock Tamson's Bairns: Essays on a Scots Childhood* edited by Trevor Royle, she describes her early years as a child of the 'Stafford Cripps' Age of Austerity [born] at the bleak end of 1947' to parents recently demobbed from the army at the end of the Second World War (*JTB* 112). She and her parents lived first of all with her grandparents and uncles and aunts on her father's side, a household full of talk and arguments around the table. Then they moved to her maternal grandparents' house, where her grandfather told her stories and sang songs and her grandmother 'said poems. Long storytelling poems' (*JTB* 115). Perhaps it was these early overcrowded years before her parents were allocated a house of their own which instilled in her her love of language and voices, which made her the dramatic poet and playwright she became in adult life. She has said 'I think my drive is towards storytelling, recording voices, exploring ambivalences ... what attracts me is the shifting point, the caught voice, anything which momentarily illumines the ways of the heart, the life of the soul' (*M* 72-3).

Liz Lochhead was educated at Newarthill Primary School, then at Dalziel High School in Motherwell. She was interested in writing, in acting and painting. Art eventually became the activity most important to her and in 1965 she went to Glasgow School of Art to study drawing and painting. Her other talents were not easily pushed aside, however, and while working on her paintings she also began to write poetry. By the time she left Art School she had already written over half of the poems which would be included in her first collection *Memo for Spring*, published in 1972. In 1971 she won the Radio Scotland Poetry Prize with the poems 'Revelation' and 'Poem for Other Poor Fools', both included in *Memo for Spring*. She taught art in various schools for eight years until 1978 when she went to Toronto as the Scottish part of the first Scottish Arts Council/Canadian Writers Exchange Fellowship, thus making the move into life as a full-time professional writer. Her second poetry collection *Islands* was also published in 1978, with the third *The Grimm Sisters* following in 1981.

From the first, Lochhead's poetry was marked by its story-telling quality, even when a poem was not strictly what one would call a narrative poem. It was also marked by its dramatic nature, that ability to communicate the voices and personalities of the speakers in the poems, to create dramatic scenes or episodes. It is not surprising, therefore, that eventually she began to write performance pieces, dramatic monologues and eventually works for the theatre. Her collected poems from *Memo for Spring* to the mid-1980s were published in 1984 as *Dreaming Frankenstein and Collected Poems* and this was followed in 1985 by *True Confessions and New Clichés*, a collection of her dramatic mono-logues and other performance pieces.

In addition to her performance work, Lochhead had been experimenting with plays for the theatre since the early 1980s, working with companies such as Wildcat, Borderline Theatre and Scottish Youth Theatre. *Blood and Ice*, based on Mary Shelley's *Frankenstein*, was performed at the Traverse Theatre, Edinburgh, during the Festival in 1982 and *Dracula* at the Royal Lyceum in Edinburgh in March 1985. An adaptation into Scots of Molière's *Tartuffe*, commisioned by the Lyceum, was performed at the Lyceum in January 1986 and in Glasgow during Mayfest the same year.

Lochhead has said that *Tartuffe* was a very important play for her since it was here that she first found herself using Scots language in a play: 'But to my great surprise it was in actual Scots, most of it. It wasn't a decision. It wasn't just English for Scottish speakers. It was Scots, and then that led to setting it in the 1920s.' And then, having discovered 'this well that I didn't realise was there, of even vocabulary, and definitely thought and rhythm' she found that it 'was available for *Mary Queen of Scots Got Her Head Chopped Off'* (*TV* 126).

Mary Queen of Scots Got Her Head Chopped Off was commissioned by Communicado Theatre Company to mark the 400th anniversary of the death of Mary Queen of Scots and was first peformed at the Lyceum as part of the Edinburgh Festival Fringe in 1987, where it won a *Scotsman* Fringe First award. Since then Lochhead has continued to write poetry together with drama and performance work for theatre and radio. *Bagpipe Muzak*, published in 1991, contains all three aspects of her work. *Mary Queen of Scots Got Her Head Chopped Off* was published in book form by Penguin in 1989 and has remained one of the most popular of her plays with audiences as well as with the author herself, a work she has called 'a metaphor for the Scots today' (*LLV* 162).

2 Mary Stuart and her Historical Background

Mary Stuart (or Stewart as the name was originally) was born in December 1542 at a point of extreme crisis in Scotland. Her father James V had just been defeated at the Battle of Solway Moss by the forces of King Henry VIII of England who wished to bring Scotland under his own control and out of the orbit of Catholic France. Many Scots, nobles and commoners, were killed in this battle and many who survived found themselves taken to England as prisoners of King Henry. James himself suffered a severe physical and mental collapse after his defeat and died six days after the birth of his daughter in despair over the future of his kingdom. 'It [i.e. the Stewart rule of Scotland] cam wi' a lass and it'll pass wi' a lass', he is reputed to have said when the disappointing news of the birth of a daughter was brought to him on his deathbed (Mitchison *HS* 99). John Knox put the situation more tersely with his 'All men lamented that the realm was left without a male to succeed' (Fraser *MQS* 11).

The political situation at the time of Mary's birth in 1542 was critical in two important and related areas. Firstly, there was the traditional hostility between Scotland and her more powerful and prosperous neighbour England, given fresh impetus by Henry VIII's break with the Roman Catholic Church and his fears that Scotland's 'auld alliance' with Catholic France might provide a backdoor route into England for the Roman Catholic rulers in Europe who wished to depose him and restore Catholicism.

Related to this political/religious power struggle was the crisis in the Roman Catholic Church itself. Throughout Europe the Church had for long been seen as corrupt and in need of reform. By the time of Mary's birth dissatisfaction had gone beyond reform to the establishment of a new Protestant form of Christianity and in Scotland there were already religious reformers committed to this new way forward, although Scotland officially remained a Catholic country until 1560. The growing religious conflict within Scotland itself, where Protestant reformers were confronted with a Catholic monarchy and the strong influence of the Catholic French Guise family, therefore added to the tensions caused by the on-going enmity between Scotland and the newly Protestant England. Amid all this, the fate of the child Mary took on symbolic significance. In 1548 the balance of influence clearly became French when, a marriage having been arranged between Mary and the heir to the French throne, she sailed from Scotland to France at the age of six to be brought up in the court of her future in-laws, as was the pattern of the time; and also, most probably, to escape the danger to herself of the violent incursions into Scotland by the English which had restarted during 1545-48.

Mary remained in France until 1561. Her husband Francis had been crowned King in September 1559, but had died in December 1560. At the age of nineteen, therefore, Mary returned to Scotland to take up her role as Queen of Scots.

As she had left Scotland at a time of crisis, so Mary returned to her throne at a critical period for the country. The Queen Regent, her mother Mary of Guise, had died in 1560 and the Scottish nobles were vying with each other for power. The Scottish Reformation was now a *fait accompli* with Roman Catholicism outlawed by Parliament and John Knox denouncing the Mass from his pulpit in Edinburgh. The official adoption of Protestantism by Parliament inevitably brought the country closer to Protestant England and its new Queen Elizabeth, whom Mary had already alienated by insisting on her own right to the English throne.

Despite her inexperience of Scotland and her difficulties with John Knox, who had written in the time of Mary of Guise's Regency against 'the monstrous regiment [rule] of women', Mary's rule in Scotland appeared initially to promise well. The turning point came with her marriage in 1565 to Henry Stewart, Lord Darnley. Like Mary, he was of Catholic family background and also had a claim to the English throne through their common grandmother Margaret Tudor, daughter of Henry VII. Whatever the motivation for their marriage – political interests or passionate feeling – Mary's attraction to Darnley soon waned, especially after the murder of her secretary, the Italian musician David Riccio, a murder in which Darnley was believed to be implicated. After the birth of their son, the future James VI of Scotland and I of England, there appeared to be a brief reconciliation between Mary and Darnley before he in his turn was murdered in an explosion at Kirk o' Field House, Edinburgh. By this time Mary's control over her factious country was slipping. She turned for help to James Hepburn, Earl of Bothwell, a strong-minded nobleman who was believed by many to have been involved in the murder of Darnley. Mary's subsequent marriage to Bothwell increased the opposition to her in the country and caused her nobles to take up arms against her. She was defeated in battle and fled south to ask for refuge in Elizabeth's England.

Mary's request for asylum presented Elizabeth with a difficult situation. Mary had always insisted on her claim to the English throne and might therefore provide a focus for the hopes of rebellious Catholics if she remained in England. Yet if she were to be returned to Scotland, she might well be killed.

Mary remained imprisoned in England until her death in 1587. During that period she did, either unconsciously or at times consciously, act as a focal point for rebellion against Elizabeth. Eventually, after the Babington plot in 1586, in which she was implicated, she was put on trial and found guilty. She was eventually beheaded, after much procrastination on Elizabeth's part, at Fotheringhay in February 1587. In 1603, after Elizabeth's death, Mary's son, James VI of Scotland, succeeded to the English throne.

Many explanations have been offered as to why the reign of Mary Queen of Scots turned out so disastrously and tragically. Some commentators have seen her as an emigrée queen at the mercy of feuding Scottish nobles and a Scotland she could not understand. Some have blamed her failure on the fact that she was a female sovereign trying to operate in a rigidly patriarchal society; yet that did not inhibit the success of her cousin Elizabeth of England. Religion has been seen as the source of the disaster with a Catholic queen at the head of a fiercely Protestant country. Viewed from opposing religious perspectives, Mary has come down to us through the myths of history either as a martyred madonna or an unscrupulous sexual adventurer, a magdalen figure. The poet Edwin Muir depicted her in a BBC Scotland Radio programme in 1942 as a queen *predestined* to disaster because of the circumstances of her upbringing: 'already far away/stretches the road that leads to Fotheringhay'. And he added: 'She was in the net before she set foot in Scotland'. More recently the historians Ian Cowan and Jenny Wormald have argued that Mary's downfall was brought about by 'her own political ineptitude'. For Cowan, 'she remains a tragic figure caught up in a situation which was beyond her capacity' (Cowan *MQS* 30). Jenny Wormald is harsher. In her *Mary Queen of Scots: A Study in Failure* (1988), Wormald finds 'a monarch of little wit and no judgement .... What I have found is someone neither "bad" nor "mad", but simply very sad' (Wormald *MQS* 8).

3 Lochhead's Approach to Mary and her Historical Background

The above details of Mary's life are important for an understanding of Lochhead's approach in her play. Liz Lochhead is faithful to the *facts* of Mary's life as they have come down to us through history. Apart from La Corbie and the symbolic characters, Dancer and Fiddler, the principal *dramatis personae* are the players in the actual historical drama – Mary, Elizabeth, John Knox, Riccio, Darnley, Bothwell. The pattern of Mary's life and relationships follows the historical pattern, as does the pattern of Elizabeth's life as Queen of England. Lochhead has said that she found this the most difficult of her plays to write, although she now considers it her best: 'first it was the worst. I mean, I was the most panic-stricken, kept putting off the actual writing doing research, research, more research on it' (LLV 10). This research enabled her to make her modern reader or audience aware of how the conventions surrounding queenship and marriage in the late medieval period might have conditioned the conduct of both Mary and Elizabeth, female sovereigns in a strongly patriarchal culture. Given that the norm was a *male* sovereign, queens became queens usually through marriage and so queenship, characteristically, was dependent upon and consequent upon marriage. In addition, the subtle relationship between sovereign and subject, where the monarch had on the one hand to be seen as 'unique' and on the other to be 'representative' of his people, accessible to them, was often expressed in the metaphor of marriage. The king, it would be said, was like a husband to his people and they were subject to him, just as a wife is subject to her husband. (Similar symbolism could operate in the religious sphere, where the church was spoken of as the *bride* of Christ.) A queen could also act as an intermediary between the king and his people. She could provide an appearance of accessibility through her beauty and virtue, which allowed her husband to maintain his sovereignty and uniqueness, without appearing aloof from his people. It was an almost impossible task for a female sovereign to operate within these conventions on her own. Yet if she took a husband, as Mary did, she could find that her own status as sovereign was diminished. Lochhead succeeds in creating a historical context in her play which makes Mary's anxiety to marry and Elizabeth's contrary determination not to give up her female sovereignty equally credible and equally debilitating in their different ways.

What is most significant about Lochhead's play, however, is that it presents the story of Mary's short reign in a manner which encourages the reader or audience to think critically about – to interrogate – the historical evidence and the way in which the historical sources have been interpreted and communicated over the centuries; and, very importantly, to consider how these historical happenings and interpretations – these myths even – have conditioned our lives in the present time.

Lochhead has said of her early poetry, 'my country was woman' (*PPP* 23) and much of the impact made by collections such as *Memo for Spring* and *The Grimm Sisters* was due to the fact that for the first time in Scottish poetry, readers were being confronted by poetry of high quality written about women's lives and women's perceptions of our human world, and written *from the inside* by a female poet using a modern idiom, in which metaphorical language and imagery was drawn from female experience. This poetry was an outstanding challenge to the male-dominated poetry tradition of Henryson, Dunbar, Burns, MacDiarmid, Muir, MacCaig *et al* and a challenge also to what its author considered to be the strongly patriarchal nature of Scottish society, even in the later twentieth century. Despite that early focus on woman, however, social concerns and involvement with country were always part of the context of Lochhead's poetry and in the 1980s she began to bring gender and country more explicitly together in her work, a move which was to result in the *Mary Queen of Scots* play. Therefore, while the focus of the play is to a large extent a gender one, featuring the two queens, Mary and Elizabeth, the relationship between them, their conduct of the role of sovereign and the consequences of this for each, it is a play which also explores themes of religion, hypocrisy, personal and national identity, self-delusion and self-knowledge and, to a certain extent, class relations. In all of these thematic areas, we are encouraged by the methodology of the play to investigate and separate out myth from reality, to open up our minds to alternative interpretations of our past and therefore of our present, so that we can move forward.

Nowhere in the play is this approach more challenging than in the presentation of the religious dimension of Mary's tragedy and the way in which this Roman Catholic/Protestant division has etched itself into the very psyche and institutions of Scottish society. Although Lochhead's ostensible subject is the Scottish religious division of the late sixteenth-century, her exposure of intolerance and certainty of rightness is equally relevant to the Scotland of our own time, as well as relevant to non-Scottish situations such as the Troubles in Ireland, the civil war in the former Yugoslavia, the Palestinian/Israeli conflict and many others. Lochhead has written of her Protestant girlhood in Lanarkshire where, although her parents were unbigoted, she was conditioned by the separate religious schooling system and the country's religious culture generally to consider the Roman Catholic tradition and Mary Stuart in a negative way. In adulthood, however, she found herself reconsidering Scotland's history and looking at a demonisation of Mary Queen of Scots which seemed to her to be linked to the dethroning by the Protestant John Knox of that other Mary, Maria Regina, Queen of Heaven. As La Corbie, the black crow 'chorus' figure of the play comments sarcastically after a difficult interview between John Knox and Queen Mary: 'He has cowped the Queen o' Heaven, so how could he worry 'bout cowpin' a mere earthly queen?' (23). For Lochhead the contemporary poet, this cowping of the two Marys has led to a suppression of the female principle in Scotland and the beheading of Queen Mary thus seemed to her an act which symbolised this wider suppression of the feminine in Scottish life and art.

All these themes and approaches to themes will be explored in detail as we move into the play itself. At the outset, however, it is important to be aware that Lochhead's *Mary Queen of Scots Got Her Head Chopped Off* is not a historical pageant or 'illusion of real life' kind of play, but a play which challenges us to look critically at ourselves, female and male, at our attitudes, our country, our history, our religion. It is also, as one would expect from Liz Lochhead, a highly entertaining, witty drama.

Before we move into the discussion of the play itself, here is a brief note about forms of drama and performance styles in drama which may help us more readily understand the dramatic methodology adopted by Lochhead and what she achieves through this.

4 A Preliminary Note on Dramatic Form and Performance Styles

Broadly speaking, the history of stage drama can be divided into three phases. First of all there is the period from the early classical Greek drama of Athens in the late sixth century B.C. to the open-air European drama of the fifteenth and sixteenth centuries. This phase included medieval miracle and morality plays such as the English *Everyman* play and the mid-sixteenth-century Scottish *Ane Satyre of the Thrie Estaitis* by Sir David Lindsay, together with the rise of the Elizabethan theatre of

Shakespeare and his fellow Renaissance dramatists. Although specific details varied throughout the timespan and from culture to culture, in this early kind of drama no attempt was made to represent everyday life in a naturalistic way, although the passions and conflicts portrayed were recognisable human dilemmas. The emphasis was on role-playing, on stylised language and signs of drama (such as masks in Greek drama, for example) and on an imaginative collaboration with the audience in bringing the stage presentation to life.

Private theatres came into being in the early seventeenth century and the productions of this second phase of drama were marked by the indoor nature of the presentation and a more naturalistic style of performance which sought to portray characters and happenings in a way which approximated to the 'real life' of its bourgeois or upper class patrons. This led to a less interactive relationship between audience and stage – a situation encouraged by the new style of theatre with its proscenium stage, curtains and seating arrangements.

This naturalistic form of dramatic presentation is still very much with us in the twentieth-century, especially in television drama, but in this century a third kind of dramatic production has also been prominent. This most recent phase in some ways looks back to the first period in that it has deliberately turned away from an illusionistic or naturalistic performance style towards an emphasis once again on the *means* of representation, on performance as *performance*. We find this form in an early twentieth-century modernistic play such as W. B. Yeats's *The Dreaming of the Bones* (a symbolic drama about the troubles in Ireland), in plays by Samuel Beckett such as *Waiting for Godot* and *Endgame* and especially in the dramatic productions of Bertolt Brecht in Germany during the 1920s and 1930s. Working as he did in the years after World War One and during the rise of the Nazis in Germany, much of Brecht's drama had a social and/or political agenda and his expressionistic style of performance was deliberately conceived to encourage his audience to interrogate what was happening in society and politics and to participate in a *critical* way in the scenarios being acted out on the stage as opposed to passively identifying with preconceived ideas as in the more naturalistic, illusion-of-real-life drama. When putting forward his ideas about theatre, Brecht insisted:

> Do not allow a fourth wall to divide you from the
> audience ... Let the audience see you are not this

> character, but you are an actor representing this character and that you do not necessarily agree with what your character is doing/saying ...

And again:

> When you go on stage imply what doesn't take place as well as showing what does. Try to show that instead of moving down left – you could have moved up right. Instead of saying 'You'll pay for that' you could have said 'I forgive you'. (BT 136-40)

This making an audience aware of the possibility of alternative actions and interpretations, of the possibility of exercising choice on the part of a character, is an important element also in Liz Lochead's *Mary Queen of Scots Got Her Head Chopped Off.* She has said that what led her to accept the commission from Communicado Theatre Company was their 'whole expressionistic, epic, story-telling, anachronistic, *non* "fourth wall" direct-to-the-audience style of *presentation* (rather than "acting")' (*LLV* 160). Her dramatic method therefore calls on approaches such as Brecht's *Verfremdungseffekt* – the 'making strange' effect, or 'alienation' effect, as it is sometimes called in English, which operates through presenting a character or a happening in a way that leads the audience to think freshly about what is happening on stage, to question opinions and actions. The effect is achieved through the use of *Gest*, non-verbal performance details which might involve visual or musical material, costuming or a particular kind of physical movement, something we will see in action in the John Knox scenes of the play.

In Scotland, drama was brought to an abrupt end by the Reformation and the hostility of the reformed church to stage performance. While from the eighteenth century onwards it began to make an appearance again, it is really only in the twentieth century, and especially in the post-1945 period, that theatre companies with a Scottish agenda have flourished. What is interesting about these small companies – Wildcat, Borderline, Communicado, the Scottish 7.84 company and others – is that they have chosen to operate to a large extent through a Brechtian or other non-naturalistic mode of performance, thus making a link across the centuries with that lost earlier tradition represented by David Lindsay's *The Thrie Estaitis.*

5 Lochhead's Approach to the Dramatic Presentation of Mary and her Historical Background

As mentioned above, *Mary Queen of Scots Got Her Head Chopped Off* was commissioned by Gerald Mulgrew and Communicado Theatre Company to mark the 400th anniversary of Mary Queen of Scots' death in 1547. This was the start of a complicated process to produce what Lochhead has described as one of the most difficult of her plays to research and write. The draft play was workshopped by Communicado between May and July 1987 and this workshopping process resulted in more research, more reinterpretation and restructuring. The working manuscripts and typescripts of the play, held by the National Library of Scotland in Edinburgh, provide fascinating documentation of a continuous creative process over the months, building up to the first performance in which ideas essential to Lochhead's view of her subject gradually find their final form in a stage composition which is eclectic in its dramatic styles and anachronistic in its handling of historical time.

Lochhead's play is therefore very different from a pageant history or endorsement-of-historical-reality type of drama. Her approach is *eclectic* in the sense that she makes use of a variety of presentational styles. From its first words, 'Country: Scotland. Whit like is it?', spoken not by a historically dressed human character, but by La Corbie – '"the crow, the corbie, le corbeau, moi!" ... an interesting, ragged ambiguous creature' (11) – the audience is invited to ask questions, to become involved in the action, to try to work out what is going on. Lochhead's use of non-verbal signs of drama works to a similar end. Music, dance, pictorial detail, anachronistic costuming, animal references and interchangeability of characters all emphasise the *role-playing* nature of the drama, emphasise that it is not an illusion of reality, but a constructed and subjective version of historical events which is itself open to scrutiny and reinterpretation. This dramatic methodology allows us as readers and theatre audience to question traditional representations of historical characters and happenings. For example, in Act I scene 4 John Knox is presented by the stage directions as if he was a bigoted member of the Orange Order. '*Knox is ranting*' and behind him '*two men, stamping, sway a big sheet like a blank banner behind him, swagger on the spot with exaggerated Orangeman's gait*' (19). This is an example of the Brechtian method of *Verfremdungseffekt*, the 'making strange' effect. The traditional presentation of Knox as hero of the Reformation is 'made strange' to us and we are brought to think about religious intolerance – past and present – and how bigotry and hatred can be part of a supposedly righteous, moral position. The stamping of feet, the banner and 'Orangeman's gait', the 'hoochs and ugly skirls' and the anachronistic visual detail such as bowler hat, umbrella and the Orange Order references themselves are what in Brechtian drama is called *Gest* – a difficult word to translate into English, but a word which means a gesture or other performance detail which communicates the essence or gist of the action to the audience. On the other hand, the more naturalistic presentation of the interview between Knox and Mary in the latter part of Act I scene 4 leads to the realisation that Roman Catholic and Protestant religious beliefs are both *interpretations* of biblical teaching and neither can be proved or disproved as the true Word of God.

Mary herself has been most often portrayed by sympathetic writers as a victim, as someone fated to be destroyed by the situation of a Scotland from which she had been absent for so long. We find this view in Nancy Brysson Morrison's biographical and fictional accounts of the queen's life and, as mentioned previously, in the broadcast scripts Edwin Muir wrote for the Scottish BBC in the 1940s. Lochhead's portrayal departs from this stereotype. Although she is on the whole sympathetic to Mary, her ironic, non-naturalistic presentation and the way in which she constructs actions which show Elizabeth and Mary responding in very different ways to the same proposals and challenges, make us aware of *choice*, of the fact that, as Brecht taught, characters *could have done otherwise*, and that we as human beings, whether historical or contemporary, can take a hand in our own destiny.

The following are some of the principal elements of dramatic presentation, the *signs of drama* which we will have to take account of in our working with Lochhead's text.

Stage Directions
In drama generally, these can be minimal or expansive, depending upon the nature of the play being presented. They may merely be concerned with organisational details such as how actors enter and exit the stage, to whom they address their speeches and where they position themselves on the stage. With more development, stage directions may comment on the nature of a character's mood, perhaps with suggestions as to how that mood may be communicated through gesture and movement.

For readers of Lochhead's play – and many of us first come to the play as readers – the stage directions are an *essential* part of the text. They should not be passed over quickly in the wish 'to get into the text itself'. They guide us in our approach to the dialogue and action and should be followed scrupulously in performance. The stage directions will be considered in more detail in discussion of individual scenes in the play. They are important in all scenes, but are especially so in the opening scene of the play 'Scotland, Whit Like?', in the scenes which operate through the Brechtian 'making strange' effect referred to earlier, including the scenes with Knox, and the final *Jock Thamson's Bairns* scene of Act II.

Dramatis Personae – The Characters
There are nine characters listed in the Dramatis Personae section of the published Penguin edition of the play, although in the first performance at the Edinburgh Festival Fringe in 1987 there were ten, Robert Dudley, Earl of Leicester at this point still having a speaking role, as opposed to being referred to through conversation and mime as in the Penguin version. Six of these characters are actual historical figures: the Queens Mary and Elizabeth; John Knox; James Hepburn of Bothwell; Henry Darnley and Riccio, whose role is doubled by the actor who plays Dancer. Lochhead is faithful to the history that has come down to us in the roles she gives these characters, although, through her presentational method, she encourages us to view their actions from new perspectives. In additional to their historical roles, the actors playing Mary and Elizabeth double as Bessie and Marion, maidservants to the queens, and as two tough teenagers, Leezie and Mairn, in Act I scene 6. The roles of Dancer and Fiddler are outside the historical storyline and are related primarily to the use of dance and music as non-verbal dramatic signs. They appear with the historical characters, however, as twentieth-century street children in the closing scene of Act II, Dancer doubling here with Riccio to become Richie. The most unusual and arguably the most important character in the play is La Corbie whom Lochhead described in *Rough Magic*, Perth Theatre Company's Programme for their performance of the play, as 'an immortal, a "spirit of Scotland", a then-and-now sardonic, beady-eyed chorus figure in the form of a talking crow'. La Corbie acts as a chorus figure in the play, commenting on the action. She does not confirm the values of the community, however, as happens with the chorus in early Greek drama, but questions received ideas and values in a Brechtian way, either by commenting ironically on them or by directly challenging them. She is most often positioned on the

periphery of the action, commenting on it, foreseeing, when the
characters do not, where their choices and behaviour will lead.
She is also a character in her own right: a ringmaster setting the
play in motion and putting the characters to their various roles in
Act I scene 1; having the last word of the play in Act II scene 7
and in various scenes contributing to the dramatic process
through conversation with Mary, through her ballad singing,
through her presence as a kind of grannie figure, pushing baby
James in his pram in Act II. By the nature of its historical
material, the fate of women is foregrounded in this play and we
notice that the crow figure is *La* Corbie. Similarly, what it means
to be Scottish is an important motif in the play, and La Corbie is
an ever-present reminder of Scottish identity, with her name
which calls to mind the ballad of 'The Twa Corbies', her reductive
wit which brings the characters down from their self-regarding
pedestals, her understanding of Scottish culture, past and
present. La Corbie is an irreverent, involved participant in the
drama, challenging received values from within.

Song
Song is significant in the play. As mentioned above, La Corbie's
songs – or at some points declaimed verses – are especially
important, either as comments on the action or as a means of
making a transition between scenes and so moving the action
forward. Her songs are closely related to various aspects of
Scottish culture, at times evoking the sixteenth-century *Gude and
Godly Ballatis* of the Reformed Church, at others traditional
ballads such as the ballad of 'The Twa Corbies'. In scene 6 of Act
II, as she wheels Baby James she sings the everyday lullaby 'Wee
Chookie Burdie' which has shoogled many Glasgow and West of
Scotland bairns to sleep. La Corbie's singing, therefore, has a vital
part to play in the bringing together of the *diversity* of the
Scottish experience over the centuries, while at the same time we
recognise in her and in that diversity what Lochhead called a
'spirit of Scotland'.

  Song, in the form of street songs, skipping rhymes and other
song-games, is a principal dramatic medium in the final scene of
the play also, acting metaphorically as a kind of recapitulation of
the various themes and motifs of the play – the power struggles,
the longing for love, envy, female vulnerability and religious
bigotry.

  In contrast, one of the most moving episodes in the play, where
for a moment irony, political manoeuvring, envy are laid aside, is

communicated through song. This is the singing of the Wedding Song in Act I scene 8, begun by La Corbie, taken up by the whole company and ended by Mary herself in fine verses whose imagery expresses a woman's thoughts on love and marriage.

Non-Verbal Performance Detail
This includes instrumental music (as opposed to song as discussed above), dance, symbolic mime, pictorial stage composition as in the reference to the *'Brueghel Grotesques'* in the stage directions for Act I scene 6, anachronistic props such as Elizabeth's polaroid snapshot of Baby James, Riccio's paper aeroplanes, John Knox's bowler hat. Other symbolic references or actions include La Corbie's ring-master's whip and the parading of her 'circus animals', the headless doll during Elizabeth's nightmare in Act I scene 5, Bothwell's sexual mime with Bessie, the transformation of characters such as the change between Mairn and Mary in the street scene. Some of these details operate as *Gest* – signs which communicate the essence of the meaning of a happening. What we notice is how, most often, these performance details are used for *ironic* purposes, to subvert a particular action or point of view or to point forward towards disaster to come as with the 'mad tango' in the Suitors scene (12) or Dancer's snatching away the sheet at the end of the Wedding scene. These various non-verbal signs of drama are brought together most powerfully in the Brechtian presentation of John Knox in Act I scene 4 and Act II scene 4.

Language
The play is remarkable for the range of language registers it encompasses. Lochhead uses Scots and English in a variety of forms from colloquial speech to educated and formal discourse. French is introduced during the scene with the ambassadors and Mary herself speaks Scots with a French accent. In addition to this variety of language registers for communication purposes, there is also the poetic or imagistic language of the play which furthers our understanding of its themes and characters.

At the lower end of the English scale are the commoners in Act I scene 2 who show all the conventional mistrust of foreigners: 'I 'ates the bastern Spanish Spanish bastards!' (13). At the higher are the exaggerated diplomatic flourishes of the ambassadors who come to pay court to Queen Elizabeth. With the exception of the nightmare scene, where she reverts to the speech of childhood, Elizabeth's speech always has a formality about it, even when she is in intimate conversation with her gentlewoman. This queen never forgets that she is the one in command. Elizabeth can also be wittily and wickedly playful, in a consciously exaggerated way, as we see in Act I scene 2. It is not for nothing that Lochhead has described her as 'a sort of bad pantomime queen', although she quickly adds: 'I wasn't trying to send her up any more than Mary' (*TV* 127).

It is, however, Lochhead's *range* of Scots language which is most exciting. Asked by an interviewer about why she used the mixture of languages and language registers present in *Mary Queen of Scots*, she replied: 'Well, it's about Scotland and England, so obviously ...' and then added significantly: 'Everybody in Scotland at that time, even the nobles, spoke Scots'. And talking about her adaptation of Molière's *Tartuffe*, she commented that 'Scots is a fantastic language for multiplicity of register. There are all kinds of very, very local and particular class and almost gender and certainly geographical ways of speaking' (*TV* 126, 125).

This acceptance of the universality of spoken Scots and the awareness of its versatility are reflected in the language contexts of the play. Mary speaks Scots with a French accent – 'Mary didn't learn to speak in English. Mary came to the Scots' (*TV* 126). The Earl of Bothwell moves freely between registers. He speaks an educated 'sturdy' Scots to John Knox (whose language, by contrast, is very Anglified). His communication with the queen can be formal also, but most often his switching of registers during audiences insinuates, especially in Act I scene 5, a mocking, undermining element into his responses. As we will discuss later, Mary, unlike Elizabeth, speaks mostly in a personalised, intimate register which her Scots language enhances. Her maidservant speaks in a more colloquial way, with almost a countrified comforting nuance in her speech. The Scots commoners in Act I scene 2 are every bit as insular in their attitudes as their English counterparts, although the expression is now recognisably Scottish colloquial: 'They say Don Carlos isnae a' there .... Neither was her first wan, the Frenchy' (*MQS* 15). Leezie and Mairn in Act I scene 6 and Jock Thamson's Bairns in the final scene of the play are tough, wee Glasgow/West of Scotland street children with their vulgar repartee, skipping rhymes and Band of Hope songs. The 'hardmen' Mummers in Act II scene 5, with their understated violence and threatening ironical patter, provide another recognisable West of Scotland register. La Corbie, the 'chorus', whom Lochhead characterised in 'Rough Magic' (Perth Theatre programme) as a 'spirit of Scotland' appropriately has the full range of Scots registers within her power including a register which operates through the imagery and rhythms of poetry.

This employment of a language register more associated – in the modern period at least – with poetry rather than stage drama, is another striking aspect of Lochhead's play. Although her work as a whole has moved between poetry on the page and performance pieces, she has always insisted on the difference between these two *genres* and on the primacy of her poetry. On the other hand, she has said that writing certain speeches in *Mary Queen of Scots* used the same kind of energy and gave her the same kind of satisfaction as writing poetry; and she referred in particular to La Corbie's opening speech and to the later talk between Mary and La Corbie 'about the Virgin Mary being pulled out of the sky in Scotland, that bit was satisfying like writing a poem'(*TV* 119). As we consider the various scenes of the play, we will at times examine language in the way we do when reading poetry, and it is through this register of poetry, both in the text itself and in the stage directions, that the moods, the characterisations and the ironic subversions of situations are often communicated. Linguistically, this is a very rich and mobile play and a study of its language will provide a reliable guide to an interpretation of its themes.

THE PLAY

Before beginning to work through the following commentary/
discussion on the individual scenes of the play, make sure that
you have read the play in its entirety at least once and preferably
twice. While reading the commentary, have the relevant scene
open in front of you so that you can bring your own ideas to the
discussion. Act One will be dealt with in some detail, scene by
scene, in order to establish both the performance styles of the play
and the major themes. There will be a reasonably detailed
discussion of Act Two also, but with the principal focus on key
scenes and a more brief discussion of others.

ACT ONE

Act One consists of eight scenes which cover the story of Queen
Mary from the early period of her return from France to Scotland
up to the point of her marriage with Henry, Lord Darnley. It
introduces the rivalry between Elizabeth and Mary, their
curiosity about each other and the difficulties each queen
experiences in her attempt to rule as a female sovereign in a
strongly patriarchal society. Mary's difficulties with the religious
reformer John Knox are also a principal feature of this Act.

Scene 1: Scotland, Whit Like?
The opening scene in any dramatic production is usually a
significant one. It is here that the audience first catches the
nature of the drama about to be presented: tragedy or comedy;
realistic in its performance style or symbolic or subversive in a
non-naturalistic mode. It is here too that the themes of the drama
and the 'characters' of the principal characters are first signalled
to the audience, to be developed more fully as the play proceeds.
      As discussed earlier, the stage directions are extremely
important in the play, and in this opening scene it is Lochhead,
the poet, whose choice of words immediately conditions the acting
space: '*Alone, FIDDLER charges up the space with eldritch tune,
wild and sad, then goes.*' There is expectation, ambiguity,
suspense created here through the directions; a sense of doom, of
potential tragedy, perhaps, and an imaginative association with
Scottish folk culture through the fiddle tune. This association is
continued when La Corbie, the 'chorus' appears, '*an interesting,
ragged ambiguous creature in her cold spotlight*' (11). She is

ambiguous not only because of her ragged crow-like appearance, but also because she enters the stage as if into a circus ring, with whip in hand, a performance detail which will be expanded later in the scene. Her significance in the first section of the scene is in drawing our attention to the *kind* of drama which is to be unfolded, pointing us towards possible themes and towards its non-naturalistic, non-illusion-of-reality performance style.

Let's begin by reading the first section of La Corbie's opening monologue from 'Country: Scotland. Whit like is it?' to 'my belly thinks my throat's been cut' at the top of page 12 of the Penguin text. Notice how this first section of La Corbie's speech is itself divided into two parts. Lines 1 -12 throw out questions about the nature of our country Scotland and what we notice is the variety of *Scotlands* which emerge – 'bricht bere meadow or a park o' kye'; 'a tenement or a merchant's ha''; 'Princes Street or Paddy's Merkit'. There is no *single* image of Scotland imposed, as so often in accounts of Scottish history and culture. Diversity or plurality, is immediately acknowledged. Yet La Corbie's words also suggest that we, the readers or audience, are involved in the creation of this complex of Scotlands. From the beginning the audience is drawn into the drama, as opposed to being kept at observer's distance. We are being asked to think about the Scotland we individually belong to and how we would characterise this: 'Ah dinna ken whit like *your* Scotland is. Here's mines'. And in the second part of this opening section, La Corbie goes on to give us her own personal, subjective view of Scotland.

Given that La Corbie appears to be acting as a kind of chorus, or mistress of ceremonies in regard to the play, and therefore as someone who can take an overview of its action, it is not surprising that her view of Scotland contains myths and truisms, clichés and cultural references that we recognise as shared perspectives. Look closely at her portrait and see what you can identify. The 'national weather' is easy; few would disagree with that! What about the others? And what is the *tone* of La Corbie's view of Scotland? Ironic? A suggestion that national identity and beliefs perhaps need some interrogation? Whatever we decide, it is clear that her views are communicated with verbal and rhythmic vitality, with wit and a sense of involvement in her task, and in a demotic or everyday Scots register which is exhilarating to listen to or to read aloud.

Having established herself dramatically, La Corbie takes up her ringmaster's role and '*cracks whip for THE ENTRANCE OF THE ANIMALS*', the *dramatis personae*. Here we have the principal characters in the historical story to be performed, but these are presented to us in a manner which immediately subverts their historicity and the expectations that we bring to the play from our knowledge of history – a manner which in addition foregrounds *role-playing* and theatricality as opposed to presenting an illusion of real life.

As La Corbie takes the actors playing Elizabeth and Mary by the hand, parading the queens before us, we notice how her language register and manner of delivery alter. Although the language is still Scots, it is more formal, less conversational; the delivery is rhetorical and expansive as befits La Corbie's *public* story-telling role here as she gathers together the elements of the historical drama and presents it to the audience, drawing that audience into the expanded circle of her telling: 'Once upon a time [the traditional story-telling beginning] there were *twa queens* on the wan green island ...' We recognise the outline of the story, although contrasts are simplified and exaggerated for dramatic purposes. Then the closing lines, with their references to the queens and their suitors, together with Dancer's 'sad or ironic jig', move the action forward into scene 2 where the rivalry between Elizabeth and Mary and the *implications* of the sovereignty of *queens* are acted out.

To sum up: What is most significant about this opening scene is that it signals that this is not going to be a historical pageant type of drama, or one which attempts to give the illusion of real life in a historical context. On the contrary, role-playing and performance are foregrounded. In addition, we are made aware of the diversity of living experiences and of the way in which our own subjectivity, our own personal experience and point of view, conditions the interpretations we make. We, the audience or readers, are therefore being prepared to explore the instability of 'historical truth', the implications of myth-making. Having, in a Brechtian sense, woken up her audience, implicated them in this opening scene through La Corbie's dramatic method, Lochhead is ready to move more acutely into the exploration of themes relating to gender, political power structures, religion and national identity.

Scene 2: The Suitors

According to historical sources, Mary and Elizabeth never met. Historians have speculated about the possible outcome of such a meeting had it ever taken place; and romantic novelists, dramatists and film makers have invented confrontations between the queens. In scene 2 Lochhead cleverly *does and does not* bring about a coming together by the device of placing each queen on a raised dais at either side of the stage and by highlighting in turn the action relating to each. Since she also brings a procession of ambassadors to each, often with more or less the same proposals for foreign marriages and alliances, we learn much about the characters of the queens from their differing individual responses to these proposals. The scene is played to what the stage directions call '*a mad tango, to music*': an ironic performance detail which reinforces the role-playing, subversive nature of the scene.

Language: One of the first things we notice about the playing of this scene, especially if we are a listening audience as opposed to readers, is the range of language registers in use and the effect of these on our interpretation of the happenings. Try reading the scene aloud – by yourself if necessary or better still with a group of fellow students – and note down what you hear and how you respond to what you hear.

The ambassadors on the whole speak a formal English where the elaborate phraseology – 'To the most esteemed royal court of Her Majesty Queen Elizabeth of England' – and the rhetorical flow of the sentence structure characterise the importance of the mission and the supplication to the queen addressed (while pointing up also, perhaps, just what an artificial, role-playing activity such missions are). Ambassador 4 addresses Mary in a mixture of French and English, perhaps a device on the part of Lochhead the dramatist to keep us in mind of Mary's French connections. The language difference which is potentially most significant in relation to the development of the action is that between the two queens. Throughout the scene, Elizabeth uses a confident, formal English style which is without the rhetorical flourishes of the ambassadors but has a *playfulness* in word-choice which emphasises her consciousness of the political game which is underway, while it signals also that she is very much the one in command. Her 'Our *bloody* dead sister's widower?' [my italics] is both a clever lowering of register for emphasis and also a pointing to her awareness of the unsavoury history behind the proposal in relation to the reign of her half-sister Mary Tudor – Bloody Mary – which makes that 'We think *not*, Cecil ...' inevitable (13). There is an even stronger example of Elizabeth's playing with language for effect in her instruction to her chief Minister of State: 'do contrive to keep the ambassador dangling. Do dandle the odd demi-promise ...' (13). We enjoy Elizabeth's wit here as the alliteration causes the rhythm to swing about in a titillating way, like the scurrying to and fro of the ambassadors. This is a woman thoroughly in command of her situation and her use of the royal 'we' maintains her distance even while she appears to be accessible to the ambassadors and the offers they put before her.

Mary is presented very differently. She speaks Scots, not English, '*a French-woman speaking Scots ... with, at the beginning of the play, getting subtly less as it proceeds, quite a French accent*'. Mary's cultural displacement, her lack of rootedness in relation to her position as Queen of Scots and to the languages and (by implication) politics of the British Isles, is therefore signalled early in Lochhead's dramatisation. In addition, her use of Scots lends a tone of intimacy to her responses, despite her status as queen; and this intimacy is present also in her subjective responses to the marriage proposals being made to her. While Elizabeth's eye and ear are always on the politically acute response, Mary would appear to be motivated by what she holds personally dear, as, for example, a *Catholic* suitor: 'At least he is a good Catholic, even if he's not a king in his own right' (13). She seems to be easily taken in by appearances, believing in the goodwill of the suitors, believing what they tell her and what she wants to believe. Even the preposterous offer of Henri de Valois as husband provokes only the mild, surprised response: 'My own Francis's wee brither! But he's no' thirteen year aul' ... How could ma belle-mère think o't?' (13). In conclusion: while Elizabeth comes out of this scene as a woman adept at playing politics and a woman well aware of the danger to her supremacy should she take any suitor at all as husband or name a successor, Mary presents herself as a womanly woman, a woman seeking marriage as a necessary fulfilment of her female and queenly role; and a woman whose marriage choice, when made, will be based on personal desire, not political contrivance.

This early opposition in the presentation of the two queens is significant for the dramatic events which follow on from scene 2. In addition, the scene itself is highly entertaining. The subversive irony of the 'mad tango' is patterned in the speed with which the ambassadors present and *re*present their suits to the two queens. The formality of the ambassadorial presentations is also undercut by the very colloquial interpolations of English and Scottish commoners, who may differ in language, but demonstrate similar insular 'anti-foreigners' points of view. As the scene moves onwards, the ambassadorial speeches become shorter and shorter and the *re*presenting of suits follows ever more quickly, adding an element of farce to the artificiality of the whole enterprise, while the Scottish nobles fight among themselves over Mary's possible marriage partner. Only Elizabeth keeps a cool, scheming head. Throughout the scene La Corbie, the chorus, watches, occasionally putting in an ironic comment, as when Mary's naive admiration of the portrait of Don Carlos is mocked by Dancer's parodying of the '*grotesque cripple*' Don Carlos is in reality (14).

At the end of this scene La Corbie restates her scene 1 description of the two queens on the one island, but this time her words evoke a different response. Heard in the context of the scene we have just witnessed, La Corbie's words have lost their neutral 'beginning of the story' quality and have taken on an ironic colouring from the play-acting, cynicism and power-seeking displayed in the scene, however entertaining it has been. We sense that scepticism and ironical perspectives are going to be needed for the interpretation of *this* story, an intuition reinforced by La Corbie's final 'Caw, Caw, Caw' (15).

Scene 3: Queens And Maids

The emphasis on role-playing continues in scene 3 with the actors playing Queen Mary and Queen Elizabeth alternating as the maids to the queens. The political manoeuvrings of scene 2 introduced implicitly the dilemma faced by both queens: how can a queen satisfy both the demands of her role as monarch and her personal needs as a woman; and this dilemma is now made explicit through the action of scene 3. La Corbie strikes the keynote with her ironic opening rhyme: '... I ask you, when's a queen a queen/And when's a queen juist a wummin?', while the crack of her whip signals the change of '*the hectic and garish but proud ELIZABETH*' into Mary's maid Bessie (16).

Performance Style: One notices a change of performance style here. The first part of this scene is one of domestic intimacy between Queen Mary and her maid and the previous emphasis on theatricality has given way to an approach which promotes – for a brief moment at least – an illusion of reality. This intimate style communicates a sense of truly felt emotion on the part of Mary and sympathy and encouragement from her maid. Mary's longing to meet Elizabeth, her hope that she will be friendly towards her, and her sense of disorientation in her new cold country of Scotland, even after three years, all come over strongly to us. This new naturalistic and intimate performance style encourages us to sympathise with Mary, even to experience with her in imagination her bewildered responses to her new situation:

> Three years! I mind me and the Maries oot on deck
> chitterin' in oor fine French frocks peerin' through
> the glaur o' the air for ae glimpse o' my kingdom!
> Three years and I havena seen it yet!

She continues:

> Haar fae the sea ... Cauld ... rebecks and chanters a
> pretty masque and a goldhaired bairn presents me
> wi' a filigree hert that's fu o' golden coins, new
> minted. Clouds. A flytin' fae Knox. Daurkness. A mad
> poet tries to mak' a hoor o' me. Wisps ... A revel!
> Smoke ... A banquet for the ambassador new fae
> Spain. Fog. A bricht affray in the Canongate, a bloody
> clash at the Butter Tron, a murdered bairn in the
> Grassmarket, sunshine, and a ragged, starvin' crowd
> o' cheerin' cheerin' weans jostle to touch ma velvet
> goon as I go by. My kingdom. Alternately brutal and
> boring. And I canny mak sense o' it at a' (16-17).

There is just enough detail of the past here through Mary's fragmentary memories to help us piece it together and enter into her dilemma.

After this sympathetic opening, we are catapulted by the theatricality of *'a drumbeat, or a flash of lightning'* out of our illusion of reality and intimacy with Mary into a parallel English scene where Mary is transformed into Elizabeth's gentlewoman 'modest Marian' and Mary's sympathetic maid Bessie becomes *'Elizabeth, proud queen ... on a pedestal, preening* (17). The second part of scene 3 then continues in a naturalistic mode, with Queen Elizabeth and her gentlewoman talking alone together. Nevertheless, there seems to me to be a difference in atmosphere from the previous Scottish scene.

This difference is communicated principally through language and language register. Queen Mary and her maid spoke more or less in the same intimate, conversational register, although Mary's range of vocabulary and references was wider than Bessie's. The effect created, however, was one of intimacy, of togetherness. On the other hand, although Elizabeth and Marian are playful in their talk, we are aware of a clear distinction in status and power. Elizabeth asks the questions and Marian dutifully answers them and these answers always endorse the English queen's beauty and superiority. Both women speak educated English, but Elizabeth's register is more formal. Elizabeth here appears just as impelled to talk about Mary as Mary previously was to talk about Elizabeth; but we notice that while Mary wished for a *personal* relationship with Elizabeth, Elizabeth is principally interested to find out how Mary compares in beauty and achievement with herself. She does not appear to feel herself seriously threatened by her Scottish cousin or to wish for a closer relationship with her. That scornful laugh on the part of Marian, when she tells her mistress that Mary writes poems 'in "Scots"', communicates to the audience the English view of the comparative status of the two nations, their cultures and their queens.

The closing sections of Elizabeth's and Marian's exchanges are significant also. We have previously heard Mary tell Bessie of her longing for marriage, something she seems to believe is essential if she is to carry out her reign properly: 'I want to marry, Bessie, I want to marry and begin my reign at last' (17). In the English setting, on the other hand, we hear Marian hesitantly proposing to Elizabeth that she should marry her lover the Earl of Leicester so that gossip will be silenced and the queen will 'live in happiness, that England shall be a peaceable kingdom' (18). Elizabeth, however, is always the politician, even in matters of love: 'I have always said I shall marry – if I marry – as queen and not as Elizabeth. You think because my subjects love me as their queen they'll have me marry where I will?' (18). Nevertheless, Elizabeth's closing thoughts, spoken as an aside to herself – 'Robert Dudley, my darling, my Lord Leicester ... my love' (19) – allow us for a moment into her private emotions, bringing to the foreground the dilemma of how to live successfully as queen and happily as woman. This question of public and private roles in relation to gender is one of the principal themes of the play and one which transcends its historical time in its relevance to the lives of ordinary women today. Mary's inability to separate out these roles, her attempt to rule as a queen with personal womanly values (a comment spoken by Elizabeth in an early draft of the play held by the National Library of Scotland is 'I hate her for trying to be a woman-queen!') is, in Lochhead's interpretation of the historical events, one of the principal reasons for her downfall. Yet, as the closing lines we have just read suggest, and as we will see more fully developed in scene 5, Elizabeth's suppression of her womanly nature in order to keep her political power intact is destructive to her wholeness as a woman. Some idea of the importance Lochhead places on this *continuing* dilemma of the suppression of the female principle can be gauged from the pre-publication drafts of the play where, even as late as the first performance at the Edinburgh Lyceum, there existed a strong scene between Elizabeth and Leicester where the demands of personal love as opposed to public power were argued out directly with much emotion and deep feeling.

Scene 4: Knox And Mary

In the opening section of scene 4 we have one of the most striking of the play's performance styles, a Brechtian approach using the techniques of *Verfremdungseffekt* and *Gest*. As mentioned previously, Brecht's aim – and the aim of Gerry Mulgrew and his Communicado Theatre Company – was to involve the audience as participators in the drama being presented; to lead them to question given situations and to realise that things could be other than the way they are, that circumstances can be changed. The 'making strange' effect is an important dramatic tool in this respect while, as always in Lochhead's play, careful attention to the stage directions is essential.

Before investigating further the implications of the stage directions, let's think for a moment about John Knox and his historical context. As we know, Knox was one of the most important figures in the Scottish religious Reformation of the mid-sixteenth century. He was influenced by the ideas of the French Protestant reformer John Calvin who had established himself in Geneva in Switzerland and he introduced Calvin's ideas into Scottish Reformation theology. Knox wrote *The History of the Scottish Reformation*, he encouraged literacy among ordinary people and for many Scottish Protestants over the centuries he has been a religious hero. Scottish Catholics, on the other hand, who were made outcasts in the new Protestant social and religious order, have viewed him less favourably. Many Scottish artists have also responded with hostility to Knox, holding the Reformed Church with its narrow moral views and distrust of human creativity largely responsible for the destruction of music, visual art and folk traditions at the time of the Reformation and for the weakening of Scottish artistic culture over the centuries since. Writers including Robert Burns and James Hogg and in our own time Edwin Muir, Iain Crichton Smith and Robin Jenkins have all condemned what they have seen as the authoritarianism and moral hypocrisy encouraged by Calvinist ideology, in addition to its restrictive effects on the creative imagination. Liz Lochhead, a female writer in a still largely authoritarian and male-dominated contemporary Scotland, presents Knox's overthow of the Virgin Mary and his contribution to the troubles which beset Queen Mary as acts which initiated a suppression of the female principle in Scotland, something which in her view has affected adversely both women and men. Scene 4 therefore not only continues the play's interrogation of gender issues but brings forward also for inspection the religious theme which is equally significant in any investigation of the condition of Scotland. As the methodology of the play makes clear, however, this is *one particular* interpretation of Scotland's religious past, not *the only* interpretation; and as discussed in the introductory material, Lochhead has deliberately chosen to turn the historical tables and examine Knox and Mary from a perspective which does not endorse the traditional Protestant view.

Let's return now to the stage directions at the beginning of Scene 4 and consider how the Brechtian approach encourages us to look with some suspicion at what is about to take place. These directions are very precise in their description of several *Gests* – or non-verbal performance details – which should be carried out to establish a frame of reference which will communicate the essence of the scene. First of all, there is John Knox himself on a pedestal *'marching'*. Accompanying him we have two men *'stamping,* [who] *sway a big sheet like a blank banner behind him, swagger on the spot with exaggerated Orangeman's gait.* In addition to these physical *Gests*, there is a musical one: *'Music and hoochs and ugly skirls'* (19).

The effect of word choices such as *stamping, swagger, Orangeman's gait, hoochs and ugly skirls, ranting*, whether read on the page or seen and heard in performance, is to arouse associations of prejudice and bigotry, mob intimidation, fear, ugly social behaviour. For the theatre audience, without the aid of the text and its *'Knox is ranting'* direction, the character of John Knox, dressed in *'bowler hat and with umbrella'* may well at this opening moment be unrecognisable as the historical John Knox of Scottish religious tradition. When he begins to speak, however, his words strike us as familiar, especially that 'blaw the first blast o' the trumpet against the monstrous regiment o' women' (19). And when he speaks, the performance details or *Gests* signalled in the directions come together with his words to create *Verfremdungseffekt*. For what is happening here is the 'making strange' of the traditional 'religious hero' interpretation of John Knox and an opening up of another interpretation of his 'religious' zeal and his certainty that God is on the reformers' side against Catholicism and against the 'monstrous regiment' or rule of women. Because of the suspicion aroused by the opening *Gests*,

when Knox speaks we are ready to notice that his words, although
ostensibly preaching the gospel of Jesus Christ, have in them that
ugly violence and prejudice already presented to us in the stage
directions. Knox's 'preaching' is seen in this context as nothing
less than a prejudiced rant, a point reinforced by the alliteration
in his closing phrases which brings the whole speech to a climax
of vicious, emotional hatred: 'the vanity and iniquity of the
papistical religion in all its pestilent manifestations in Sodom
priesthooses and poxetten nunneries' (19). The venom is literally
spat out through the alliterative plosive consonants. This is
Verfremdungseffekt at its most powerful.

As we have seen already, another dramatic method employed
in this play is an abrupt change of setting or performance style
either within the same scene or between consecutive scenes, a
juxtapositioning of styles which furthers the dramatic process and
expands our understanding of what is being presented. After the
shocking opening of scene 4, a lighting change and redeployment
of individual stage furnishings transport us to an audience
between Knox and Queen Mary where the performance style is of
a more naturalistic nature. On the other hand, the earlier
Brechtian presentation of John Knox remains in our imagination
so that we pay careful attention to the conversation between him
and Mary. What is immediately evident is Knox's *certainty* of
rightness and his utter intolerance and contemptuous dismissal of
any position contrary to his own. Although he claims to be the
instrument of God, there is none of the humility of God's servant
in his words. Lochhead communicates this authoritarianism not
only in the denotative meaning of the words he utters, but also
through the rhythms of his sentence structure, which are rigid,
leaving no space for flexibility of thought.

The manner of Mary's characterisation is interesting also as is
the *sound* of her speeches. Her language is much more *Scots* than
Knox's, which, despite the occasional Scottish word, seems
English in its structure. This might remind us of Knox's long
years spent in England, of his wish for alliance with Protestant
England rather than Catholic France, and his introduction into
his Reformed Church of a vernacular bible in *English,* not Scots,
an act with far-reaching implications for the maintenance of the
Scots language and of literature in Scots. For all her French
upbringing, Mary appears the one who is closer to Scottish
concerns. The rhythmic flow of Mary's speech gives the impression
of one human being speaking to another, as opposed to a sovereign
interviewing a subject. She appears genuinely puzzled by the

hostility shown her by Knox and seems to be seeking a
conciliatory way forward. Mary presents no threat to Knox in this
portrayal and her behaviour and demeanour are utterly at odds
with his hysterical outburst about the monstrous rule of women.

Mary is not all womanly quietness, however. She is well aware
of Knox's actions against her mother, the Queen Regent, and
against herself; and she is knowledgeable about the scriptures he
claims to hold dear. She misunderstands Knox deliberately in his
'Jezebel' references, thus putting him in a false position with
regard to Queen Elizabeth. Most importantly, this exchange
between Mary and Knox, set in the context of the opening
Brechtian parodic parade, leads the reader/audience to the
understanding that Knox's pronouncements with regard to God's
will and the certain truth of the reformed religion are no more
than one *interpretation* of God's will, and, given the language in
which the pronouncements are expressed, a bigot's interpretation
at that.

In the end, however, Knox overwhelms Mary by the brutality
of his language as he denigrates what he sees as the idolatory of
the Mass. There is another element in Lochhead's characterisation of Knox here, brought out not only by his ugly sexual
language in relation to women and Catholicism, but also by his
response to Mary's weeping. We sense in him a fear of women, of
female sexuality – perhaps a fear of his own sexuality. In his
opening rant Knox had shouted against 'Sodom priesthooses and
poxetten nunneries' and his attack on the Mass is heavy with
covert sexual symbolism linked to a sense of uncleanness. When
Mary breaks down sobbing, the stage directions tell us: *'Knox is
uncomfortable, genuinely. Stirring of certain pity, perhaps lust'*
(22). Lochhead has suggested that the suppression of the female
principle in Scottish society since the Reformation has resulted
not only in the marginalisation of women in society but has
resulted also in men suppressing the *anima*, the female part of
themselves, so that caring human qualities are regarded as
effeminate and therefore qualities to be suppressed. In this scene
we also have the suggestion of 'genuine' pity becoming confused
with 'lust' as a consequence of an unhealthy, inadequate response
to women and to sexuality, an inability to regard women in any
way except as sexual objects, a motif which will be developed later
in the play in relation to Knox's and Bothwell's response to Queen
Mary.

One further element to be considered in this scene is the role of
La Corbie. Up to this point, La Corbie has appeared outside the

action of the play, either as chorus, commenting on the action, or as ringmaster, setting the 'circus' in motion, effecting the transition from one scene to another. During the exchanges between Knox and Mary in scene 4, she maintains her chorus role but directs her comments more pointedly towards Mary as if inciting or encouraging her. In particular, the speech beginning 'Corbie says by the love of your beloved mother you must destroy this man' reinforces the hostile impression of Knox already communicated, while it emphasises the danger for Mary that he represents. This speech by La Corbie may well be one which communicates more through being *read* than being heard, since it is through our eyes that we can more quickly take in the full impact of the punning on Knox's name: 'Knox' then 'nox', Latin for the Scots 'nicht', then 'nox' linked to the idea of the noxious in 'bitter pousons', 'nox' linked to the 'three fearful chaps' or knocks on the door. La Corbie's playing on Knox's name builds up a crescendo of destruction here, before she cuts him down to size again with her ironic, dismissive '"The Guid Lord says, and I agree wi' him!" Hark, Cark Cark' (20).

After the departure of Knox, La Corbie appears to move out of her chorus role and into the drama, becoming almost a confidante of Mary in a question and answer exchange. It is an exchange which reinforces our sympathy for Mary and our perception of the destructiveness and arid arrogance of Knox. The passage 'He has cowped ... without your heavenly yin' (23) is one which Lochhead has described as giving her 'the same kind of satisfaction as writing a poem' (*TV* 119). In it she brings together opposing images which work together to strengthen our sympathy for Mary against the destructiveness of Knox: the beauty of the 'celestial blue goon' contrasted with the trampling in the muck and mire; the Virgin's traditional role as a source of comfort to those in danger contrasted with the 'black hole, a jaggit gash, *naethin'* '. The reference to mothers is a poignant reminder of Mary's childhood without her mother and her current wish for a loving relationship to sustain her – a wish which brings the scene to an end with Mary's return to her preoccupation with marriage and her insistence that she will marry for love and not for political reasons.

Scene 5: Repressed Loves
Despite its impact and significance in terms of the themes of the play, scene 4 is a fairly short scene. Scene 5 is more than twice its length and provides a set of variations on the theme of sexuality and queenship. In particular, we see here the consequences of

Elizabeth's suppression of what La Corbie calls 'her womanische nature' (23).

There are two parallel actions in this first part of the scene. Elizabeth's dilemma is played out simultaneously in 'real time' as we see her lie in a disturbed sleep and in 'dream time' through symbolic mime and music. The 'real time' nightmare communicates Elizabeth's genuine agitation and fear as opposed to her previous queenly role-playing; while the symbolic mime acts out the possible psychological reasons for such distress with stage props of beheaded doll and stolen crown – signifiying, perhaps, her memories of her beheaded mother Anne Boleyn and her fears of losing her own power as queen if she were to follow her feelings and marry the Earl of Leicester. The part of the scene involving Elizabeth ends with her once more in control: 'I am proud that loving him, still I will not let him master me' (25).

The transition from Elizabeth to Mary is made through La Corbie's ironic rhyme, which suggests that marriage is a 'chancy' business for any woman and through another symbolic mime, this time involving the Earl of Bothwell as huntsman with Dancer performing the Highland stag dance. As in the scene between Queen Mary and John Knox, there is a sexual element in the interview between the queen and Bothwell who has been accused of rape and appears to see all women – queen and commoners – as his sexual prey. Mary tries to exert her authority in insisting that 'in my realm ... women should sleep sound in their beds'(26), but Bothwell disregards her, continually returning to sexual innuendo. This is especially evident in the fine piece of prose poetry beginning 'In the chase? Aye. When there's a fine white hind dancin' afore me through the trees ...' (27-8). The imagery and the rhythmic movement of the lines create the effect in this tensely erotic passage, especially when read aloud or spoken on stage. The stressed syllables of 'fine white hind' are followed by the flowing movement of 'dancin' afore me through the trees'; then there is a hide and seek pattern, a speeding up in the short phrases separated by commas: 'and I glisk it, then lose it again, glisk it, lose it ...'. 'My hound, my pointing hound' is sexually suggestive, with the vulnerability of the quarry emphasised by the emphasis on baying and smelling and 'glintin' through the trees in the gloamin' daurk'. The whole passage moves in the pattern of a chase. The scene ends with a mime in which Mary's sexual attraction to Bothwell, as yet unrecognised by herself for what it is, is demonstrated by means of a symbolic 'lewd' kiss, which reaches the queen via her maidservant Bessie. This sexuality motif is continued into the final part of the scene through Bessie as she is transformed into Queen Elizabeth who is now plotting to send the young Lord Darnley to Scotland in the hope that he will attract Mary and so solve the problem of a safe marriage for the Scottish queen.

Scene 6: Mary Queen Of Scots's Progress And John Knox' s Shame

In scene 6 the actors playing Mary and Elizabeth are transformed to Mairn, '*a wee poor Scottish beggar lass*' and Leezie '*her tarty wee companion*'. Both appear as part of a crowd of onlookers cheering Queen Mary's progress through her capital city. We don't see the Queen herself, the focus being on the crowd '*in love with royalty and splendour*'. As always the stage directions are important: '*Bright professional music from shoulder-high fiddler .... The whole set of Brueghel grotesques is cheering*'(32).

Lochhead's poetry and performance work has always shown a strong understanding of the ordinary everyday culture from which she herself comes; and with this understanding goes the artistic capacity to find exactly the right word and performance detail to give it form. The stage directions for this scene 6 could be seen as operating as *Gest*, for all the elements appear to work together towards presenting the scene's communication of the *complexity* of human responses to the experiences they share. The superior status of the queen, her mystery and magic for those who watch, is communicated by that instruction for 'bright *professional* music', while the cheering, excited crowd demonstrates our capacity to be taken out of our humdrum, sometimes painful lives, even for a brief moment, by entering into an out-of-the-ordinary experience. The final instruction in the opening directions: '*The whole set of Brueghel grotesques is cheering*' is very important. The mid-sixteenth century Flemish painter Brueghel is famous for his *genre* paintings, his scenes of ordinary, everyday life which can simultaneously be full of bright colour, laughter, mischief and the 'grotesque' – both in the sense of human physical abnormality, such as Lochhead's dwarf s*houlder-high* fiddler, or in the sense of 'doubtful' activities. But life itself is mixed in this way, and as scene 6 progresses, we become aware of the *aridity* of Knox's angry moral condemnation, when placed against the energy and vitality of ordinary human beings and their capacity to absorb whatever life brings their way.

Awareness of social class and of different kinds of social circumstances is characteristically present in Lochhead's poetry.

Although this is not a theme that is foregrounded in the *Mary Queen of Scots* play, it is nevertheless present in the presentation of these street children, as it is in the device of the role-changing between queens and maids throughout the play and in Bothwell's upper class exploitation of the maid Bessie, even if she does seem willing to be exploited. In scene 6 the theme of social class is touched upon when the girls admire the queen's beauty and Leezie, the more forward one, points out that they could be just as beautiful in 'braw claes' (32). Although undeveloped, it's an acute social observation which is part of the complex of responses communicated in this scene.

Comments on the eclectic or varied performance styles adopted in the play have so far been directed towards emphasising how the predominance of a non-naturalistic, non-illusion-of-reality method of presentation encourages us to view the drama in an active, participatory way; to question what we see on stage, think about its implications for the historical story being told and for our lives in contemporary Scotland. On the other hand, up to this point in the play Lochhead has encouraged us to feel sympathy for Mary by using a more naturalistic performance style in scenes where Mary holds centre stage, while the satirical, Brechtian method has been largely reserved for John Knox. Scene 6 continues to emphasise the negative implications of Knox's ideology and personal actions. Mairn and Leezie taunt Knox, provoking an uncontrolled sexually abusive outburst which is then redirected towards the queen herself. The stage directions are important at this point, contrasting the energetic vulgarity of Leezie – '*a flashed bum*' – with the shocking stillness of the frozen tableau as Mairn transforms into Queen Mary and the complexity of Knox's emotions towards the queen is caught in that direction '*Knox's hand raised in anger but stayed in awe*'(33). After the shock of that stilled moment, it is impossible to read or listen to Knox's foul-mouthed, sexually violent verbal attack on Mairn without recognising it as expressing his *irrational* feelings towards Catholic Queen Mary. The contrast between the word choices and imagery in his outburst against Mairn/Mary and his closing 'Pray God forgive you and sin nae mair' (33), leads one to ask who, in a truly life-giving sense, are the sinned against and who are the sinners here.

La Corbie pushes this message home in a Brechtian manner with her song 'In papische days wi' evil ways' which is then repeated by the whole company. Her song reminds us that one impulse behind the Protestant Reformation was the corruption of the existing Catholic church and clergy, their sexual licence and lack of education, their sale of indulgences and their disregard of the people's everyday needs. If you have read the fourteenth-century Chaucer's *Prologue to the Canterbury Tales* or David Lindsay's *Ane Satyre of the Thrie Estaitis,* written and performed around the 1550s, close to the historical events of Lochhead's play, you will be familiar with perceptions of this religious decline, presented by Chaucer through comedy and by Lindsay in a mixture of performance styles and registers in several ways similar to the theatrical methodology of Lochhead's play. La Corbie's song about 'papische ways' appears to suggest that while the religious ideology may have changed, human impulses and actions are not so easily altered. There is still corruption among churchmen. The scene ends with Knox continuing to denigrate Mary, this time through dismissive gossip with the Earl of Bothwell whose attitude to women is conveyed through the coarseness of his language. La Corbie effects the transition to the final two scenes of Act I and the marriage of Queen Mary with Darnley by means of a song which this time points to the Queen's lack of rationality in emotional matters as she comforts Darnley on his sick bed.

Scene 7: Darnley and a Fever
This is a short scene, not quite two pages in the Penguin text, and an apparently quiet, uneventful scene. Yet it is important in the way it prepares the atmosphere for the final scene of Act I, the wedding of Mary and Darnley. As so often in the play, language register is significant. Mary's Scots language gives a warm, personalised tone to her utterances. Darnley's English is more formal, even distanced, as if he found it difficult to communicate in a personal way. In addition, Mary speaks to Darnley with an active friendliness; she speaks in the way childhood friends speak to each other after a long parting, catching up on news; or in the way one might speak to a new acquaintance with whom one immediately strikes up a strong rapport. Her speech is a complex of friendliness, mothering, child-like enthusiasm, and all with an enjoyment of being needed. It may be that Lochhead deliberately exaggerates the *domestic* tone of Mary's responses here with her breathless 'it's me. It's Mary!' and her closing 'I brocht you some broth! I forgot! That wis why I came! It'll be cauld noo, I'll go get some mair' (35). We see Mary here not as the queen but as the lonely wee girl she was and still is, happy to have someone to care for, someone to need her, someone to love. We have an inexperienced, childlike

Mary here, virgin despite her widowhood, and more than ready to fall in love with Darnley. On Darnley side, his 'public-school' formality and his lack of easy talk with women emphasise his youthful inexperience also, as does his talk of his mother and 'junkets and milk jellies and broth to get my strength back up!' (35). The effect of this kind of exchange between Mary and Darnley could well have been mawkish or even mocking. Yet, while one might smile a little at their naivety, there is a poignancy in their developing love which keeps cynicism at bay. For a moment we are spectators at a scene of genuine attraction between two young people who need each other and the fact they are queen and aristocrat, as opposed to two ordinary people, makes no difference to their need, as La Corbie earlier reminded us in her scene 3 rhyme: 'when's a queen a queen/And when's a queen juist a wummin?' In case we become too sentimental, however, Lochhead breaks into Darnley's 'Just ... stay with me, Mary' with a sudden scene and style change which brings the entrance of Elizabeth 'puffing on a clay pipe' (36). This visual *Gest* is sufficient to let us know that Elizabeth's plans have succeeded. We hardly need the self-congratulatory soliloquy which spells out her triumph in detail.

Scene 8: A Wedding

Scene 8 presents yet another performance style, proceeding as it does through symbolic mime and song and almost entirely without irony. All through Act I Queen Mary has been presented from a sympathetic perspective, even although as readers or audience we have been encouraged by the performance method to question her choices and approaches to her role as Queen of Scots. In contrast to Elizabeth, we have seen her make decisions from the heart rather than the head, and in scene 7 her falling in love with Darnley came over as a genuine emotional involvement, even if somewhat naive.

In scene 8, Mary's wedding with Darnley is similarly presented as a genuine loving meeting, a moment out of time, solemn yet erotic as the stage directions indicate. The scene is played through a mixture of music and symbolic mime – the laying out of the wedding sheet, the drawing of the pins from Mary's mourning clothes, the singing of the wedding song. La Corbie begins the song in ballad-like verses but without her usual caustic commentary (although the phrase '*shivery sound*' applied to her voice in the stage directions might remind us that many ballads beginning in love have an ending in sorrow). The focus, however, is on the loving pair and on the ritual making of the marriage bed as the company takes up the song. As Mary sings the final verses, each player draws out a pin from the queen's mourning clothes, thus freeing her to make her new marriage and new life. This is a very beautiful episode in the play, slow-moving, ritualistic and symbolic, erotic, a moment held by the music and the mime. Mary's verses (37-8), sung as she shakes free her long red hair, are a woman's wedding ballad, where the eroticism in the imagery comes from the woman who is the subject of her own poem; from a woman's awareness of her body and sexual being as opposed to the image being imagined or imposed from the outside by a male response to female beauty. Her verses are also very beautiful rhythmically, with the movement rising towards the end of the lines, carrying over the emotion and the image to the next line, while alliteration and internal and end-rhyme combine with the rhythmic movement to create a seductive and personalised effect.

The tension in the scene is maintained after the singing has come to an end as Mary and Darnley each take an end of the wedding sheet and 'intent on each other' slowly circle and twist the sheet into a love knot. The magical mood is then broken as *'Dancer, swift, snatches it immediately away'* (38) – an ironical *Gest* which points forward to the disenchantment to come.

ACT II

Scene 1: Seigneur Riccio, a Fortune, a Baby and a Big Baby

Scene 1 of Act II takes place about three months after Mary's marriage to Darnley and with the queen in the early stages of pregnancy. By this time the reader or audience should have become familiar with the *variety* of dramatic methods employed in the play and with the *implications* of these methods and their performance details: the fact that this is not *the* interpretation of Mary's history, but *one* such interpretation; the irony in performance detail directed at self-delusion and hypocrisy, at the power games being played with particular reference to gender and religious matters; and, in relation to the anachronistic performance detail, the reminder that the issues being presented in the historical setting also have relevance to our contemporary world. In consequence of this greater familiarity with the play's methodology, discussion of scenes in Act II will on the whole be less full than in Act I, although key scenes will still be explored in some depth.

We learn much about the kind of court Queen Mary has set up from this first scene of Act II. Riccio, the queen's foreign secretary would appear to have become indispensible to Mary, playing the Tarot cards to suit her mood, telling her what she wants to hear. Mary is already in disagreement with her new husband Darnley, a situation anticipated by Dancer in that swift snatching of the sheet at the conclusion of Act I. Now she is protesting against the kind of challenge to her authority which her more politically astute cousin Elizabeth had foreseen: Darnley has authorised a commemorative coin which places his name before his wife's. As Mary says, 'the damnable cheek of it – *Henricus* et Maria, Deo Gratia *Rex* et Regina Scotorum! Wrang order' (40).

The conversation about the Tarot cards in the scene is important for the historical information it communicates to the audience. We find out that Elizabeth has been harbouring the Scottish nobles who rebelled against Mary's marriage, although she herself had been behind the events leading to the marriage. Mary's suspicion of those who surround her in Scotland and England seems to have intensified and we see her turning towards a familiar Catholic France for solace. Yet we sense also that she can expect as little genuine help from Europe as she can from Riccio's shifting interpretations of the Tarot cards with their pattern of lovers, the devil and death. We do not see a queen in charge of her country here, negotiating with her nobles, keeping a watch on the doings of her parliament. Instead we find Mary trying to carry out her role with personalised, intimate values, with the kind of court organisation which might appear more appropriate for the Queen Consort of France than for a woman who is Queen of Scotland in her own right. A close examination of the detail of the stage directions throughout the scene uncovers the insubstantial nature of Mary's activities and of her chief adviser, Riccio. As presented here, this is a deeply insecure queen who is not in charge of her country.

As always, on the other hand, Lochhead the dramatist encourages us to feel sympathy for Mary as well as impatience with her behaviour. The syntax and rhythm of the line 'Och I widna wish for ye to be a lassie' (40) emphasises the queen's apprehension about the gender of her coming child. The rhythmic pause necessitated by the 'ch' in 'Och', the stressed syllables of 'widna wish', then the onward flow of the rhythm to 'lassie' placed strategically at the end of the line convey the queen's emotional awareness of her own vulnerable situation as a female sovereign. The human emotions displayed in the scene are complex but understandable. There is sarcasm, jealousy in the drunken Darnley's words: 'My lovely wife. My beautiful wife. D'you know she is the Queen? Therefore she must be beautiful' (43), comments which pay a mocking lip-service to the medieval convention of a queen consort's symbolic beauty and virtue, while they point also to his suspicions with regard to Mary's relationship with Riccio. Yet his following more informal comment, 'She is though', as he touches Mary's hair, seems poignantly from the heart, as does Mary's cradling and comforting him – *not bitterly* – as the stage directions make clear (44). La Corbie's closing ironic comment reinforces Mary's continuing dilemma: rather than gaining a consort and helpmate, she has 'yin big bairn, and yin on the wey!' (44).

Scene 2: Rumplefyke
In contrast to the somewhat melancholy, restrained atmosphere of scene 1, scene 2 is short, lively and splendidly vulgar with an equally passionate contribution from its two protagonists, the Earl of Bothwell and Mary's maid Bessie. What gives it much of its vitality is Lochhead's ear for language.

Bothwell and Bessie are engaged in 'rumplefyke' or 'houghmagandie' as Burns called it. Even without the help of a Scots dictionary, the *sound* of these words pushes us in the direction of meaning and both are energetically earthy. The lovers' repartee in lively, colloquial Scots is as fast as their kissing and the sounds and rhythms of the words and phrases convey the changing moods of the topics raised in their conversation. There is nothing here of the repressed sexuality and censorship represented in the John Knox scenes of the play and much sympathetic talk of Mary on Bessie's part. What we have is a recognition that sexuality is part of life, part of one's nature as a human being.

On the other hand, it seems to me that the scene is not entirely free from censure. As in previous scenes, Bothwell is presented by Lochhead as a very 'macho' character, a man who enjoys the sexual power he exerts over women, even if these women are willing lovers; a man who cannot understand relations between a man and woman which are *not* of a sexual nature, as we see from his comments about the queen and Riccio. He cannot understand Bessie's acute observation: 'Does it no' occur tae ye maybe she loo'es Davy Riccio because he is the only man wha has ever touched her *withoot* he wants tae tummle her?' (45). There is, too, something distasteful in his mocking of Riccio's deformed back, using this to create a sexual *frisson* in his wooing of Bessie. Therefore, although the scene is not judgemental in its presentation of sexual relations *per se*, I would suggest that our attention is drawn once again to the presence of a sadistic element in Bothwell's character with regard to women that does not bode well for Bessie or, as we see later, for the queen.

Scene 3: Whispers, Rumours, Souchs and Chatters

This very short scene achieves its effect principally by means of mime – a '*moving motif of laughter, whispers, passing letters, espionage*' (46) – which suggests both the continued absence of Mary from affairs of state and the rumours and plotting proliferating throughout her kingdom during her absence. We recognise performance details from scene 1 such as the typewriter, the letters to France, the paper aeroplane which is used dramatically to break into the hectic pace and bring about a moment of stillness which is then itself broken into by Mary's reading aloud of the threatening words on the paper. Although Riccio dismisses the warning, La Corbie reinforces it with her 'rumours, souchs and chatters i' the court, an' in the streets gowsters [boasters] mairch vaunty an' crawlin' chauntin' oot hatred tae the Catholics' (47), a closing commentary which leads us into the dramatic presentation of hatred and rumour in scene 4.

Scene 4: Knox and Bothwell

A successful play maintains its dramatic impulse not only through the interaction of performance detail within scenes but also through the dramatic interaction of scene against scene. Act II has to cover in a short space of time a number of important historical events which lead to the deposition of Mary, her imprisonment in England and, many years later, to her execution by order of Elizabeth. It must therefore have presented Lochhead with the challenge of how to stage these events in a way which would be dramatically economical but which would inform the audience and be true to the historical facts. At the same time, this new material would have to be related to the themes and interpretations developed in Act I. Her solution, as in Act I, is to proceed through a variety of performance styles, setting scene against scene, one performance style against another. As a result of this changing dramatic methodology, readers or audience are kept intrigued and stimulated by what is going on, while at the same time essential information about the historical events is assimilated. As we now move into scene 4, the *rumours* of treason

and mob violence in the previous scene are translated into a
Brechtian presentation of the actuality.

Act II scene 4 is a parallel scene to Act I scene 4 which also
featured the Brechtian devices of *Gest* and *Verfremdungseffekt* in
the presentation of John Knox and his hatred of Roman Catholics.
This time the 'making strange' effect involves a musical *Gest*, the
singing of 'The Good and Godly Ballad', although we also have a
more limited version of the *visual* parodic parade *Gest*, with our
'*ragged troop* [who] *swagger on like an Orange Walk ...*' (47).
Again the word choice in the stage directions is significant: the
choice of '*swagger*'; the surprise of that '*hatred*' in the phrase
'*singing out hatred in 'The Good and Godly Ballad*'. (47)

Lochhead has chosen Ballad 23 (*GGB* 49-51) of the mainly
Lutheran *Gude and Godlie Ballatis* popular in the sixteenth
century, cutting the original from thirteen verses to six and
selecting those verses in which the storyline is clearest. The
position of verses five and six is reversed so that her version ends
with the strong message that 'the pape is the fox, Rome is the
rocks/That rubs us on the gall' (48), thus providing a link with the
previous scene's rumours about 'hatred to the Catholics'. The
metaphor of the ballad is the hunt and the identities of hunter
and hunted are clearly communicated: 'Jesus oor King is gane
hunting' (47) and the fox to be hunted is the Catholic religion and
all its adherents. *Dynamic*, the gradations of loudness and
softness employed in the ballad singing, is the most important
element here. At first the ballad is sung by the whole company,
but 'quietly, as if distant'. Then stanza by stanza the dynamic
increases alongside the evolving story of the 'cursit fox' who
devours the 'young and tender lambs'. When we reach the final
stanza the dynamic is 'louder than ever' and is now accompanied
by 'stamping' as in the Act I parodic parade (47-8). Heard on the
stage, this is a terrifying experience of being absorbed into, taken
over by the intensity of the sound and, by implication, by the
message of hatred. It is a very powerful musical *Gest* which
communicates the intolerance, the hatred, the *contagion* of the
activities rumoured in the previous scene.

Knox is made part of the powerful satirical effect by his
association in previous scenes with the Orange Walk parade and
its sentiments of intolerance and hatred and by his emerging *from*
the crowd of singers at the end of the ballad *in his recognisable
character of John Knox*. Yet although Knox and the Reformed
Church appear to be the principal targets of the satire in this
scene and its Act I predecessor, the laying bare of prejudice and

hatred extends more widely to include, by implication, all religious creeds – and secular systems adhered to with a religious fervour – which refuse to recognise the right of others to believe in their own way and who maintain power by violence and the dissemination of hatred. The dramatic methodology encourages us to think about what we mean by words such as 'religion' and 'spirituality' and about what kind of God it is that we worship if this is the way in which we live in His image. The violence of the language and imagery of the ballad – 'It did him guid to lap the bluid/Of young and tender lambs ... cursit fox ... cruel beast' (47) – when allied to the violence of the mode of presentation through the dynamic of the singing does indeed *make strange* our perceptions of Christ and Christianity and force us to consider how His *New Testament*teaching about love and humility, His use of the metaphor of good shepherd and sheep and His bringing in of the outcast to his circle of followers can possibly relate to the religion being proselytised here.

We find the violence of the ballad recurring in Knox's language as he gossips with Bothwell about the queen later in the scene. He seems to fear that Bothwell is allowing his sexual attraction to Mary to cloud his judgement of her and again one is aware of a suppressed or feared sexuality motif in the dramatic presentation of Knox. The opening scene of Act II presented a change in the relationship between Mary and Bothwell, with the queen apparently relying on him to keep Darnley under control. Now Bothwell supports the queen in the face of Knox's insinuations, pointing out that she has in fact upheld the Protestant reforms, having made no attempt to impose her own religious views and attending Mass only in private. Bothwell also emphasises the importance of 'sovereignty and legality', the upholding of a queen 'anointed by God' (49), and the upholding of the *Scottish* crown in the face of possible English interference. In this context, Knox's religious and gendered intolerance of Mary is given more treasonable implications. We are reminded of his inclinations towards Protestant England and his sense of his own importance and wonder where, at this point, he might find his interests to lie. Bothwell, on the other hand, is presented as loyal to queen and country in this scene, a characterisation detail which is important in relation to the presentation of his future relationship with Mary.

Scene 5: Mummers and Murderers
La Corbie has been on the periphery of the action for much of Act II, being used mostly to introduce or effect the transition between

scenes. From scene 5 onwards she returns to a more central position as commentator on the action. More immediately, however, it is the collapse of her chain of dominoes which symbolically effects the transition from the street scene between Knox and Bothwell to the subject of their gossip, Mary, who is herself playing dominoes with Bessie and Riccio as Darnley bursts in on them.

This Mummers scene is the kind of 'play within a play' that we find in Shakespeare's *Hamlet*, a piece of internal playacting which reflects and comments on the happenings in the main play. Darnley appears to be the chief instigator, controlling the introduction of the Mummers in the early part of the scene, explaining their presence as they assemble their props and announce their subject matter, 'The Mask of Salome'. Suspense and fearful expectation are built up by performance detail such as Darnley's inebriated state, the masked appearance of the players and their standing *'like stookies'* (52). The last-mentioned is a term used in a children's game meaning to stand stock still, but it can also mean sheaves of corn, short upstanding horns like the horns of a goat or a white-coloured plaster of Paris figure, a ghostly figure. All these possible meanings are brought together here with resonances of the supernatural, the uncanny. The stage directions reinforce the atmosphere: *'not at all merry but horribly sinister'* (52) which is strengthened by La Corbie's interpolation: 'Oh good, the Bible! Ah love a story with a bit of blood and guts in it' (52). What is most frightening is the way in which Mary, supposedly one of the spectators, is gradually drawn into the action, having a makeshift crown placed on her head and later being forced to read out Herod's words from the Mummers' script. Darnley, who first of all seemed to be in control of the affair, is now seen to be no more than a puppet himself, equally at the mercy of the players. The culmination is the imposing on Riccio of the part of John the Baptist, with his consequent murder.

In the context of previous discussions about the range of Lochhead's language in the play, an important input to the violence in this scene is the gallus Glasgow talk of the Mummers once the farce of the playacting is over and they are shown as the hired murderers they are. This is a very ironic, underplayed language register, deliberately feigning a comradely, even humorous tone, yet clearly intimating danger to anyone who doesn't conform: 'I wouldna dae that, young Henry ... That's no' hoo we dae things here in Scotland ... We couldnae hae it, Tam!/Neither we could, Wullie ... Behind you all the way, King

Henry, we're your men, yes sir ... Aren't we, Rab?/A' the wey, Geordie' (55). Lochhead said in her introduction to *Tartuffe* that she took her Scots language from a wide range of sources. Here she seems to be parodying the myth of the Glasgow hard man, the gangland scenario, the false 'camaraderie' of West of Scotland football rivalry with its undertones of religious bigotry. It is an unexpected but very effective register, frighteningly claustrophobic and intrusive in its introduction into the scene of courtly intimacy; and it contrasts with great effect with Mary's educated but personal Scots: 'Wha are ye? Wha are ye an wha did this?' (55); and then her 'He has killed oor maist special servant wha I loo'ed richt well' (56) – a poignant moment which emphasises Mary's powerlessness as much as the threats of violence from the Mummers had done previously. We see her as a pawn in the hands of those who wield the actual power, whoever these might currently be, a figure of ritual, important only for the heir she carries and perhaps only until the child is born. To add to the tension and confusion in this scene, while the Mummers and Mary and Darnley continue to act out their parts in the drama, La Corbie simultaneously chants a litany of the names of Scottish nobles who might well have been involved in the planning of the murder of Riccio and the threatening of the Queen. And as she chants, '*she's circling and drumming herself up with this, a quiet frenzy*' (55).

While this scene is therefore faithful to the historical facts of Riccio's murder as we know them, it goes beyond the story of Riccio, linking past and present through its language registers and performance details and opening up a wider presence in human affairs of betrayal and hypocrisy, power-seeking and violence for the sake of violence. We are especially aware of the vulnerability of women, more so when they are pregnant and when they have to live in a male-dominated culture where violence is the accepted solution to problems. The story being told is a historical one, but its implications go far beyond its historical situation.

Scene 6: Sweet Baby James, Auntie Elizabeth and a Sorer Sickbed for Darnley This Time

Scene 6 has to cover a large amount of historical ground. La Corbie is prominent in her role of ironic commentator and she is also in charge of Sweet Baby James, the heir to the Scottish throne, whom she wheels around the stage in a pram, singing '*a sinister wee song which is also a familiar Scottish west-coast lullaby'* (57). It is interesting to compare La Corbie's language and her 'Chookie burdie' lullaby with the threatening Glasgow talk of the Mummers in the previous scene. Both come out of the same West of Scotland cultural *milieu*, yet the choice of linguistic elements, the way they are put together and the tone created is different in each scene. There is an ironic awareness of violence in La Corbie's comments to the Baby James – 'Aye wha's the lucky laddie tae have made it this faur, eh?' (57) – but there's also warmth and concern and a kind of humour which recognises the violence but is not, as with the Mummers' talk, part of it.

As in Act I scene 2, the scene is played by alternating speeches and actions between Mary's court and Elizabeth's which brings out Elizabeth's unhappy envy of what she considers Mary's good fortune, but shows us, the audience, that Mary's fate is not at all a happy one. In their different ways, we see again both women suffering from their position as female ruler in a male-dominated culture. Elizabeth has come to realise that she has left it too late 'to whelp' (57) – the dehumanising of her language exposing the violence of her feelings of regret. Mary has husband and son and that son may in time have Elizabeth's throne. Mary is trapped, however, by a weak husband and by the knowledge that the birth of her son makes her less secure than before in relation to the plotting of her nobles.

There is a wealth of interactive performance detail in this scene which swiftly carries through the historical story while at the same time providing ironic commentary on it. Anachronistic detail such as the polaroid snap of Baby James transports the dilemmas of the queens into our own time, while La Corbie fuels the sinister atmosphere with her story of the moose and the foumart [ferret] and her concluding singing of the ballad of 'The Twa Corbies' with its tale of betrayal and death. A symbolic mime involving music and dance – *'a hideous anachronistic waltz'*(60) – whirls Mary from the bedside of the sick Darnley to the arms of Bothwell and Kirk o' Field House explodes as they make love on the floor. The accusatory chant of 'Burn the hoor!' leads into the ballad, sung *'not particularly full of pity'* by La Corbie as a lament for Lord Darnley (60-1). This symbolic/metaphorical approach to the historical events of scene 6 leaves the way open for the audience's involvement in the drama and for interpretation of motives and happenings. There is no fixed interpretation imposed and characters seem to have their share of blame and suffering.

The scene ends with a mixture of enigmatic actions, operating simultaneously and therefore resonating against each other. A wind blows, Knox with pail and sleeves rolled up scrubs at a spot on the floorboards, La Corbie sits shoogling Baby James's pram, *'watching the end of it all'* (61). Elizabeth is in control of herself again, ostensibly debating Mary's fate with her advisers, but communicating a sense of a decision already taken if only a way can be found to distance herself from it. As previously, the drama is heightened by the device of highlighting the queens at either end of the stage, each in her *'tight spot'* (63). While Elizabeth is deviously role-playing, Mary is despairing, recalling her earlier innocence and her disastrous alliance with Bothwell:

> Dinna think it wis lichtsomely or in love that I lay me doon wi' ye, in the daurk. Naw it wis in despair. Oh and wi' a kinna black joy I reachit oot for you to cover me and smother me and for yin moment, snuff oot the hale birlin' world in stillness. And ilka dawn I woke up wi' ye, I saw disaster a' mapped oot for me, clear as my Davy's magic cairds ... (62).

As so often in this play, Mary's personalised, intimate utterance draws our sympathy towards her even while we suspect or condemn her actions. Yet her words also communicate the *complexity* of human emotions and motivations, the utter aloneness of someone who does not know where to turn for help. In contrast, the scene ends with Elizabeth's deviousness and her declaration that her advisers would have to 'trick her' before she would consent to sign a warrant for Mary's death. The stage directions bring together Elizabeth's *'manic repetitions* [which] *begin to sound like instructions to invisible advisers'* with the speeding up of Knox's scrubbing, reminding us of Knox's earlier hostility to Mary and Bothwell's warnings against treasonable action. The directions ask: *'Is it bloodstains on an executioner's block that are proving indelible?'*, thus reinforcing our suspicions that Knox is not blameless in the disaster which has overtaken his queen (63).

Scene 7: Jock Thamson's Bairns
This final scene is probably the most difficult scene in the play so far as interpretation is concerned. Yet its prominence in Lochhead's conception of the work from its earliest stages suggests that it is in some way essential to her understanding of how her historical theme relates to our contemporary Scotland. The bairns with their street songs and skipping rhymes initially provided the opening scene of the play and this opening persisted

through several drafts until the final workshopping sessions with the Communicado cast. One obvious advantage in *beginning* the play in this manner would be that attention would be drawn immediately to the non-naturalistic performance style of the play, to its ironic context and, perhaps, to an awareness that its historical subject matter would have relevance also to the contemporary situation. On the other hand, a disadvantage might be that such a scene would not give the audience a sufficiently clear perception of what the play was going to be about, who were to be the significant characters in the drama and how these tough, contemporary children would fit in with supposedly factual historical happenings. In the end, all such demands and problems were solved by creating La Corbie as ironic commentator and ringmaster, or ringmistress, which allowed a 'once upon a time' story-telling mode to interact with non-illusion-of-reality perf-orming styles which encouraged audience participation and ironic interrogation of the historical happenings being *re*presented on the stage. 'Jock Thamson's Bairns' then became the final scene of the play.

Our initial response to this final scene might well be one of surprise and some confusion. We might reasonably have expected an execution scene of some kind to follow Elizabeth's 'Trick me. Trick me!', but no such direct depiction of Mary's ending is presented. We know from history, however, how Mary met her death and so suspense is readily transferred from Mary's execution to speculation as to how this unexpected closing scene will function symbolically in relation to the play as a whole.

'Jock Thamson's Bairns' has aroused conflicting interpretative responses. On the one hand, it is all too easy to recognise in the behaviour of the bairns the religious intolerance which has continued to be prevalent in Scotland this century, especially in Glasgow and the West of Scotland. We recognise the confident, catchy tunes of Band of Hope and Salvation Army Seaside Sunday Schools, the coded questions which determine whether a child is Catholic or Protestant (a religious and social division exacerbated even today by segregated schooling) and the reductive nicknames such as 'Pape', 'Fenian', 'left-fitter' (64). This is a nasty, vicious, bullying scene, all the more depressing for its being played out by children, traditionally associated with innocence, and children who are the *new* generation who will take us into Scotland's future. It is depressing also for the closed-minded nature of their songs and exchanges. The fact that so many of these exchanges are made by means of skipping rhymes and street song games, as opposed to more interactive dialogue, reduces the opportunity for genuine questioning and interaction. These songs have their own ritualistic question and answer patterns which cannot readily be broken into in order to conduct rational argument.

It is not surprising, therefore, that some commentators have found this final scene to be both a condemnation of religious bigotry in Scotland and a pessimistic recognition that this kind of behavioural pattern seems set to continue through a new generation; a condemnation also of the coarseness of contemporary Scottish life, its continuing 'macho' culture and reductive treatment of women. Such a pessimistic reading might even appear to be supported by Lochhead's own comment about her play in *Sleeping with Monsters* that 'it's really about Scotland, more about the present than the past, how those myths of the past have carried on into the present malaise of Scotland today … misogyny, Calvinism, all sorts of stuff like that' (SM 9).

On the other hand, it is possible to put forward a contrary interpretation of this last scene and therefore a contrary interpretation of the play as a whole. Throughout our study of the play, we have noticed how the non-naturalistic performance style and the *interaction* of the eclectic performance details have encouraged us to participate in the drama of Mary's story, to question portrayals, to pick up ironic resonances in the action. In particular we have been made aware of the emphasis on *role-playing* and on the interchangeability of roles. We have learned that *things could be other than they are*, as Brecht taught his actors to make clear to their audience.

If we apply this approach to the final scene and view the street children in a *non*-naturalistic as opposed to an illusion-of-reality mode, then rather than the stereotypes of prejudice and persecution being reinforced by the presentation of a new generation of bigots and bullies, such bigotry is diminished and mocked through the appearance of the bairns. John Knox, for example, is transformed from the frightening figure of prejudice in the Brechtian scenes of Act I and Act II to 'Wee Knoxxy', 'a loner' and his *baptism* of the others is subverted by the use of the *dirty* water from his pail (63). The suggestion earlier in the play of a psychological and sexual dimension to Knox's hatred of Queen Mary and the Virgin Mary is brought out into the open here by his obvious terror when the bairns shove his head up Marie's skirt. This reduces him from the chosen instrument of God to a sexually repressed and psychologically disturbed human being, a lesson, perhaps, that proclaimed high motives may be suspect and that we need to look more carefully for the source of narrow ideologies. Elizabeth, too, is diminished by her transformation to Wee Betty, a nasty, envious, sexually precocious girl. Indeed, all the players are knocked from their high historical pedestals, except, perhaps, Mary/Marie, who although presented as a lonely, frightened child, still retains our sympathy as a consequence of her persecution by the others and her inoffensiveness towards them.

By reducing these historical personages to vulgar, ill-educated schoolchildren, the dramatist adds further encouragement to her audience to question the status of historical 'truth' and especially the interpretation of historical happenings. Throughout the play we have been encouraged to explore themes relating to religious prejudice, political power and gender discrimination, especially in relation to the difficulty of a woman exercising public power in a patriarchally organised society and of reconciling the exercise of a public role with that of personal female and human needs. We have been made aware too of class discrimination and insularity in regard to foreigners, although these motifs have been less significant in the playing out of the principal dramatic action. We have watched the operation of hypocrisy and self-delusion, of betrayal, of the enjoyment of power over others, of violence for its own sake. But we have been incited by the performance detail to interrogate and challenge such behaviour. The employment of anachronistic performance detail, as in the 'Jock Thamson's Bairns' scene and elsewhere in the play, has certainly encouraged us to see that the play's themes are relevant in both historical and contemporary periods. 'We're a' Jock Thamson's bairns' is one of those Scottish clichés which, like Burns's 'A man's a man for a' that', seems to suggest that we Scots are without prejudice or discrimination, that we are all willing to embrace each other, welcome in the stranger. This cliché is reversed here, suggesting that we can all be 'Jock Thamson's bairns' in a more negative sense also. Yet the implications of the final scene go beyond this negative perception.

In her writing about women, Lochhead has always insisted that she criticises from the inside – 'I get at them because I'm allowed to. I'm one of them' (*PPP* 204) – and it is this *insider's* approach to Scottish history and the Scottish cultural context generally that prevails in *Mary Queen of Scots Got Her Head Chopped Off* and in the presentation of this final scene of the play. In spite of its acknowledgement that contemporary Scotland still needs to reform itself, the 'message' of the play can therefore be interpreted as potentially an *optimistic* one in the way its dramatic methodology encourages us to interrogate our past and present, to realise that neither historical nor contemporary patterns are set in stone; that interpretations can be questioned, prejudices investigated, different choices made. As Jock Thamson's bairns, we are all implicated in our history and in our attitudes to our present and future, but we can make choices, both in our personal and public lives; things do not need to be the way they are. Mary Stuart's motto was 'In my end is my beginning', a motto often reversed as biographers and historical writers portrayed her as a fated figure, predestined by her historical background to come to a sorry end. Lochhead's play could be seen as proposing that by interrogating Mary's life and her ending, by learning from it that we can choose to do otherwise, we contemporary Scots may find our own new beginning.

BIBLIOGRAPHY

Works by Liz Lochhead
Dreaming Frankenstein and Collected Poems(Edinburgh: Polygon, 1984)
True Confessions and New Clichés (Edinburgh: Polygon, 1985)
Mary Queen of Scots Got Her Head Chopped Off and Dracula (Harmondsworth: Penguin Books, 1989)
Bagpipe Muzak (Harmondsworth: Penguin Books, 1991)

Interviews and Essays by Liz Lochhead
'A Protestant Girlhood' in *Jock Tamson's Bairns: Essays on a Scots Childhood*, edited by Trevor Royle (London: Hamish Hamilton, 1977), pp.112-125.
'Liz Lochhead', Interview with Rebecca Wilson in *Sleeping with Monsters: Conversations with Scottish and Irish Women Poets* edited by Gillean Somerville-Arjat and Rebecca E. Wilson (Edinburgh: Polygon, 1990) pp.8-17.
'Women's Writing and the Millennium' in *Meantime: Looking Forward to the Millennium*, introduced by Janice Galloway (Edinburgh: Polygon, 1991), pp.71-75.
'Knucklebones of Irony', Interview with Liz Lochhead and linking commentary by Colin Nicholson in *Poem, Purpose and Place: Shaping Identity in Contemporary Scottish Verse* (Edinburgh: Polygon, 1992), pp.203-223.
'Liz Lochhead Interviewed by Emily Todd' in *Talking Verse*, edited by Robert Crawford *et al* (St Andrews and Williamsburg: Verse, 1995), pp.115-127.

Critical Background
Robert Crawford and Anne Varty, eds, *Liz Lochhead's Voices* (Edinburgh: Edinburgh University Press, 1993) includes a most useful bibliographical checklist by Hamish Whyte, together with biographical information and chapters on Lochhead's drama.
Bill Findlay, *A History of Scottish Theatre* (Edinburgh: Polygon, 1998)
Antonia Fraser, *Mary Queen of Scots* (London:, Weidenfeld and Nicolson, 1969); also illustrated abridged edition, 1978.
Emily Lyle, ed., *Scottish Ballads* (Edinburgh: Canongate, 1994); 'The Twa Corbies', p.263.
Margery Palmer McCulloch, 'Women and Love' in *The Women's Forum: Women in Scottish Literature, Chapman* Double Issue

Nos 74-5. Winter 1993, pp.46-52.

—*Sixteen Poems of Liz Lochhead,* Cassette Commentary with readings by Liz Lochhead (Aberdeen: ASLS, 1995)

Rosalind Mitchison, *A History of Scotland* (London: Methuen, 1970)

Randall Stevenson and Gavin Wallace, eds, *Scottish Theatre Since the Seventies*(Edinburgh: Edinburgh University Press, 1996)

Anne Varty, 'The Lady and the Vamp' in *A History of Scottish Women's Writing*, ed. by Douglas Gifford and Dorothy McMillan (Edinburgh: Edinburgh University Press, 1997).

Jenny Wormald, *Mary Queen of Scots: A Study in Failure* (London: George Philp, 1988).

Other Works Cited in Text

Bertolt Brecht, *Brecht on Theatre,* transl. John Willett (London: Methuen, 1964).

Ian Cowan, *Mary Queen of Scots*, Saltire Pamphlet 9 (Edinburgh: Saltire Society, 1987)

Iain Ross, ed., 'The Gude and Godlie Ballatis' (Edinburgh: Saltire Society and Oliver and Boyd, 1940)

THE ASSOCIATION FOR SCOTTISH LITERARY STUDIES
aims to promote the study, teaching and writing of Scottish
literature, and to further the study of the languages of
Scotland.

To these ends, the ASLS publishes works of Scottish literature;
literary criticism and in-depth reviews of Scottish books in
Scottish Studies Review; short articles, features and news in
ScotLit; and scholarly studies of language in *Scottish
Language*. It also publishes *New Writing Scotland*, an annual
anthology of new poetry, drama and short fiction, in Scots,
English and Gaelic. ASLS has also prepared a range of
teaching materials covering Scottish language and literature
for use in schools.

All the above publications are available in return for an annual
subscription. Schools can receive teaching materials by joining
ASLS at a special reduced rate. Enquiries should be sent to:

ASLS, c/o Department of Scottish History, 9 University
Gardens, University of Glasgow, Glasgow G12 8QH.

Telephone/fax +44 (0)141 330 5309
e-mail: office@asls.org.uk
www.asls.org.uk